FOOD ON WHEELS

THE COMPLETE GUIDE

TO STARTING A FOOD TRUCK,

FOOD CART, OR OTHER

MOBILE FOOD BUSINESS

JENNIFER LEWIS

COPYRIGHT © 2011 BY JENNIFER LEWIS

PUBLISHED BY RABBIT RANCH PUBLISHING

ISBN 13: 978-0615533667

ISBN 10: 0615533663

EDITOR BY TAMARA MILLER

COVER DESIGN BY MICHELLE DRAEGER

For Ethan

I look forward to saying "I knew him when"

after he takes the culinary world by storm.

"A goal without a plan is just a wish."

~ Larry Elder

TABLE OF CONTENTS

TABLE OF CONTENTS

TABLE OF CONTENTS

TABLE OF CONTENTS

Appendices

INTRODUCTION

Shortly after writing my first food business book, *Starting A Part-time Food Business; Everything You Need To Know To Turn Your Love For Food Into A Successful Business Without Necessarily Quitting Your Day Job*, I started a blog focused on small food business ownership titled smallfoodbiz.com. While the blog covers all aspects of the artisan and handcrafted food world, time and time again I was asked for specifics about how someone could start and run a food truck. It really should come as no surprise since food trucks are the hottest thing in the food world right now. Plus, when else have entrepreneurs been able to essentially start up a restaurant for a fraction of the price? A food truck business offers everyone, be they a trained chef or a passionate home baker, a millionaire or an unemployed cubical worker, the opportunity to start and run the business of their dreams.

As such, it only made sense to follow up with this second book dedicated to the delicious world of mobile cuisine. If you read *Starting A Part-time Food Business*, you will notice there are many similarities between the two books. This is because when it comes to starting and building any business in the food industry there are fundamentals that remain the same regardless of whether your business is on wheels or on terra firma. When it comes to mobile food businesses, though, there are a number of specific issues that arise, from permitting to parking, that have to be taken into consideration. This book will take you through all all steps necessary to start and run a successful mobile food business.

A note about how this book is organized. Most business professionals will tell you to write a business plan prior to obtaining business licenses or trying to find a place to sell your product. However, it's impossible to build a strong and reliable business plan until you fully understand all the components that go into it. This book places the business plan section towards the end with the aim of taking you through all aspects that will go into the plan before you actually write it. You may find it useful, however, to start drafting notes as you go through each section of this book so that when it comes time to write the business plan you already have a working outline you can use. A recommended Business Startup Checklist is available on page 164.

THE STREET FOOD MOVEMENT

If you're reading this book then you've likely already noticed that food trucks are popping up everywhere. Once only a common sight around places like construction sites and Hollywood movie sets, food trucks have stepped outside their normal boundaries and are essentially taking over cities across North America. And the food in these trucks is not at all like the greasy reheated tacos and soggy burgers you may remember. In a nutshell, food trucks have upped their game and now it's easy to find gourmet burgers with bacon jam, delicious Parisian-style crepes, and Jalapeno-Chocolate ice cream.

Many credit The Great Recession with helping mobile eateries go upscale and gain popularity so quickly. Chefs who could no longer get loans for restaurants, gourmet delis, and other brick-and-mortar establishments found that food trucks were a much cheaper and viable alternative. So they took their skills and experience and started serving restaurant-quality food from food trucks. The same was true for the amateur butchers and bakers who, perhaps due to an unexpected pink slip from their corporate jobs, wanted to find a way to inexpensively turn their food dreams into reality.

Along those same lines, the slowing economy forced consumers to cut back on their spending. Foodies began to search for delicious and innovative grub from a food truck at a fraction of what they would have had to pay in a restaurant and they started spreading the word.

Throughout all of this, the Eat Local Movement with its focus on eating locally-produced and sustainable food, was growing in strength. Whether it was a strategic move or simply a necessity, the early street food entrepreneurs were some of the first to jump on board and, as a collective, buy and incorporate local ingredients into their dishes. After all, food trucks, with their lower overhead costs, allow food entrepreneurs to spend more time and money searching for local ingredients. Another possibility is that food trucks, which don't need the same large quantities of ingredients that bigger restaurants do, are more able to work with small family farms to procure ingredients. Regardless, the Street Food Movement should be credited with helping bring the Eat Local concept in an affordable form to the masses.

What makes joining the Street Food Movement so attractive to many people though, in addition to the great food itself, is its accessibility. You don't need to be a trained chef to open up a food cart. Just about anyone with a good business idea, some solid recipes, and a little startup capital can start a mobile food business. What's more, the Street Food experience is palpable to the customers as well. It doesn't matter how refined your palate is or how much you make —anyone who has ever stood in line in the hot Austin sun for cupcakes at Hey Cupcake! or waited 30 minutes for duck fat fries from Phoenix-based Truckin' Good Food gets to enjoy, for a few minutes at least, the feeling of being part of a larger community. Food trucks are the great equalizer and everyone is invited to join the party.

A Note About The Street Food Movement

Though Street Food and food trucks seem like they've been a fixture in our communities for years, the truth of the matter is that the Street Food Movement has caught many cities and towns off guard. As of the printing of this book many governments don't yet know how to legislate food trucks and there are ongoing arguments over things like what health code rules govern food trucks and where food trucks will be permitted to park. While you should be aware of and keep abreast of any changes to food cart and food truck guidelines in your community, it shouldn't be a deterrent. If all the rules were already set in stone it could be argued that you had probably missed the boat – or in this case the truck – on the Street Food Movement. The fact that the rules are still a little fluid points to how early we are in the Street Food Movement and how much opportunity still exists for food entrepreneurs.

TEST DRIVE

Developing & Testing Your Menu

So you're interested in starting a food truck business. Do you know what you plan on serving? Two things make a successful food truck business stand out from competitors. First, those trucks choose to limit their menus to a few options within a well-defined niche. And secondly, they make those menu items better than anyone else.

It's possible to start a mobile food business using either your own honed recipes or by hiring a trained chef to develop and later produce all of your items. The later is certainly not necessary and will be a significant additional cost, but if you're someone who always burns toast, your dreams of a food business may stand a better chance with a professional at the helm.

If you plan on using your own cooking skills the first thing you need to consider, before you look at buying a truck or scouting out possible selling spots, is to determine what in your cooking repertoire you do better than most. Perhaps you make cookies that everyone always says you should sell. Or maybe your traditional Croatian lunch recipes are as delicious as they are unique. If you're reading this book you likely already have an idea of what type of food you'd like to sell. Regardless of what you're planning, it's worthwhile to spend time testing and fine-tuning your recipes.

During the testing process, if your recipes are not already calibrated into weight measurement, use this time to convert your recipes from "cups" to "ounces." This not only helps when you start increasing the recipes to make larger quantities, but it also makes figuring out your cost for each product or unit significantly easier (see page 95 for Product Cost Analysis information). Scales for weight measurement can be purchased from any kitchen supply store. A Recipe Testing Worksheet is in Appendix III on page 148 for your use.

These testing sessions are also a great opportunity to figure out how much prep work can be done in a kitchen and how much must be done onsite. Since part of your success will depend on feeding as many people as possible, you should consider how you can best serve customers quickly while still maintaining quality. This will also enable you to better outfit your truck or cart with the right equipment when you go to lease or buy it (more information about food trucks and food carts starts on page 33).

Along with testing your recipes, it's also worthwhile to simplify your menu. The point of mobile food businesses, and one of the things that customers enjoy about them, is that the menus are typically fairly limited. Food kiosks of all types are not restaurants and customers – who are usually standing outside in the elements – don't want to wait in the rain while everyone in front of them mulls over 45 menu items. As a food entrepreneur a concise menu means you can keep a tight rein on ingredient costs since you'll likely need fewer ingredients that will result in less spoilage and loss of product.

A simplified menu doesn't mean that you can't experiment, though. You can certainly change up items weekly or even daily as ingredients come in and out of season and you can try new menu items out on customers to see how your new ideas are received. As you develop your menu, you should plan to offer at least one vegetarian or vegan option and one or two items that you believe will sell extremely well (these don't have to be boring!) before adding in any radically new, exotic, or experimental items to test on your customers. You want to make sure that anyone who comes to your food truck or food cart hungry will find something to satisfy them.

Buying Ingredients

Depending on the size of your town or city, there may be stores in your area that cater to food professionals and with your business tax ID number you will be able to shop at those stores and take advantage of their wholesale prices with no sales tax. Another option is to open up a wholesale account with a food wholesaler like United Natural Foods, Incorporated (www.unfi.com). Companies like this will sell you ingredients in bulk sizes at wholesale prices. The only downside is that there is usually a minimum sales amount which may exceed what you need or what you want to spend at any one time. One option for mobile food entrepreneurs is to take advantage of membership warehouse stores like Costco® or Sam's Club® where you can buy items in bulk at reduced cost. A list of other places to purchase ingredients begins on page 158.

Understanding Your Customers

If you only read one portion of this book this should be it because the single most important thing you need to know to be successful in the food truck business – after knowing how to cook or finding someone who does – is who your target market is. Knowing who your customers are and what they want and need is critical. You need to understand where your customers are, you have to understand how price sensitive your customers are, and you have to understand how to best communicate with your customers.

When asked who their target market is, many food entrepreneurs will answer with "everyone loves my product." Unfortunately "everyone" is a bit of a gross overgeneralization no matter what you're selling. You simply can't make a product that will appeal to everyone.

Think of it this way, your buffalo burgers, no matter how delicious, are not likely to be high on a vegetarian's list of favorite things. Spend a few minutes thinking about your proposed food truck and you'll likely be able to identify groups of people for whom your products would be a good fit. Some common food truck customers, depending on what you're planning to serve, might include office workers looking for a quick and relatively inexpensive lunch, farmers' market or festival patrons who seek snacks made from local ingredients, college kids looking for a cafeteria alternative, or the late-night crowd in search of midnight munchies.

The best way to learn more about your potential customers — and determine if your mobile food business is something they'd be interested in — is to conduct some market research. Don't worry, it's not as intimidating as it sounds! The information you gather about your target market will be the foundation of your marketing plan. At the same time you don't want to start your business unless you are confident there's a market out there for your products.

The key to inexpensive market research is using the Internet. There is a tremendous amount of valuable research available on the Internet free of charge so it's worthwhile to start with a search and see what it yields. For example, if you're planning to start up a gluten-free food truck it might be worthwhile to do some research into how many people in the U.S. suffer from celiac disease or choose to live a gluten-free lifestyle. In addition to reports and studies, you also can surf gluten-free forums and blogs for more information about what the hot topics are in that market and what those people – your potential customers – are concerned about.

You also can use the Internet to gather additional quantitative data such as ages, gender, income level, and marital or family status for people in your local area. You can get a lot of this information in the U.S. from census reports (www.census.gov) and from similar resources in other countries. This type of data can provide you with insight about the people living in your area to determine where in your community is the best to take your mobile food business. Another valuable resource is Neighborhood Scout (www.neighborhoodscout.com). While geared more towards the real estate industry, this site breaks down demographic groups by neighborhood and can provide you with a general description about different areas that can benefit you during the business planning process. Local Small Business Administration offices and Chambers of Commerce also can be helpful as you gather information about the surrounding population.

While you can get a lot of data sitting in front of your computer, the best way to research your potential customers is ethnographic research. Don't let the fancy word frighten you – ethnographic research is essentially studying people in their natural environments. If you're thinking about taking your food truck to farmers' markets then go to the actual markets and watch how people shop. If you plan on targeting families at youth soccer games with your food cart go to a few games and see if people purchase food from onsite vendors or if they bring food from home with them. Check the foot traffic at local colleges and universities or see how many office workers downtown actually leave the office building to grab lunch. Getting into the marketplace and watching your potential customers' food purchasing habits will help you gain an informed gut instinct about your target consumers that you can use throughout your business planning process.

Competitive Analysis

The word "competitor" may not be the right one when talking about mobile food businesses because so many food truck and food cart entrepreneurs are incredibly willing to share information with one another. Because the rules governing food trucks are still in flux, many mobile business owners have banded together to try and strengthen the Street Food Movement in their area.

Despite this camaraderie, when starting a business of any type you have to know who your competitors are so you can build your business strategy accordingly. The easiest way to create a quick competitive analysis is to list out the food businesses, both mobile and nonmobile, in your area along with the type food they serve, where they're typically located, and what their biggest advantage is. The advantage may be that these establishments have a reputation for serving excellent food, for their inexpensive menu, or anything else that makes them attractive to customers. The following is an example of a competitive analysis for the fictional food truck company Sweet Bits Treat Truck.

Business Name	Food Type	Mobile Y/N	Target Market	Location(s)	Comparable	Complimentary
Sweet Bits	Gourmet Cookies	Y	children & families	Beaches & Parks (afternoons & evenings), Children's Sports Events, Festivals & Farmers' Markets		
Fish Fry	Fish & Chips	Y	families, beach picnickers	Beaches & Parks	N	Y
Burger Master	Burgers & Fries	Y	college students, late-night crowd	University area	N	Y
BBQ Shack	BBQ Sandwiches	N	families, late-night crowd	6th & Pine	N	Y
Greta's Bistro	French - Full Menu	N	couples, adults	3rd & Main	Y	N
Crab Cave	Seafood - Full Menu	N	adults	7th & Keystone	Y	N
Greta's GF Goodies	Desserts	Y	children, families, adults who like dessert	Festivals, Fairs, Farmer's Markets, 4th & Market	Y	N
Dessert Haus	Desserts	N	special-order desserts	5th & Magnolia	Y	N
Ben's Ice Cream	Ice Cream	Y & N	children, families	4th & Magnolia (N), Beaches & Parks (Y), 3rd & Capital (Y)	Y	N
The Sushi Spot	Sushi - Full Menu	N	adults, couples	3rd & Pine	N	N

As you can see, the list includes all the mobile food businesses that operate in the area whether the serve sweets or not. Sweet Bits also added a sampling of local brick-and-mortar restaurants to the analysis because they also are competitors for consumers' food dollars. If this list shows that your food idea isn't completely unique that doesn't mean you need to abandon your mobile food business dreams. Many cities have multiple food trucks serving similar items. The key in this case is determining how your truck will differentiate itself. This could be accomplished by offering different menu items, by providing a level of service the other food trucks don't have, by where and how you source your ingredients, or by the locations you visit, just to name a few options.

In addition to clearly seeing who your direct competitors are, the competitive analysis also is helpful in highlighting which trucks or restaurants might be complimentary to yours. These are businesses that you might want to work with or, if possible, park near because your menu attracts the same types of customers without cannibalizing sales from one another. In Sweet Bits' case below, the owner believes that Fish Fry, Burger Master, and BBQ Shack are complimentary and customers coming to those trucks might be looking to finish off their meal with a gourmet cookie. At the same time, Sweet Bits could provide value to those other trucks because customers who were planning to visit the truck to grab a treat and may decide to get dinner from one of the other trucks or restaurants while they're in the area.

Being able to see your competitive landscape, both the direct competitors and complimentary food businesses, will help you determine if your idea is viable and, if so, help guide your selling strategy. More about developing a selling strategy starts on page 57. In the meantime, the completed competitive analysis for Sweet Bits Treat Truck follows on the next page and a blank Competitive Analysis Worksheet for your use is on page 149.

Competative Analysis

Business Name	Food Type	Mobile Y/N	Target Market	Location(s)	Comparable	Complimentary	Differentiation
Sweet Bits	Gourmet Cookies	Y	children & families	Beaches & Parks (afternoons & evenings), Children's Sports Events, Festivals & Farmers' Markets			Gourmet baked-to-order cookies served hot
Fish Fry	Fish & Chips	Y	families, beach picnickers	Beaches & Parks	N	Y	
Burger Master	Burgers & Fries	Y	college students, late-night crowd	University area	N	Y	
BBQ Shack	BBQ Sandwiches	N	families, late-night crowd	6th & Pine	N	Y	
Greta's Bistro	French - Full Menu	N	couples, adults	3rd & Main	Y	N	High-end desserts available to restaurant customers
Crab Cave	Seafood - Full Menu	N	adults	7th & Keystone	Y	N	Store-bought desserts for restaurant customers - not handmade, not fresh
Gluten-Free Goodie	Desserts	Y	children, families, adults who like dessert	Festivals, Fairs, Farmer's Markets, 4th & Market	Y	N	Gluten-free dessert items, including cookies, main competitor!
Dessert Haus	Desserts	N	special-order desserts	5th & Magnolia	Y	N	Special occasion cakes, cupcakes, party desserts
Ben's Ice Cream	Ice Cream	Y & N	children, families	4th & Magnolia (N), Beaches & Parks (Y), 3rd & Capital (Y)	Y	N	Handmade ice cream truck, main competitor as people may want ice cream & not cookies in the summer heat!
The Sushi Spot	Sushi - Full Menu	N	adults, couples	3rd & Pine	N	N	

[31]

GETTING YOUR WHEELS

Mobile food businesses come in all shapes and sizes depending on what you need, what you plan to sell, and how much you want to spend. It's possible to start as small as a bicycle cart or pushcart, attach a food truck or trailer to your car or truck, or go so far as to purchase a full-fledged catering truck. In fact, now you can even purchase an electric hybrid food truck if you'd like to go the eco route! Understandably, the first question most people have is how much a mobile food unit will cost. For this reason, before you get your kitchen on wheels you should consider your menu and talk with your local health department to determine what rules may apply to your specific area. Some cities and towns only allow food trucks to sell food that has been prepared elsewhere which means you may not want to spend money outfitting a truck with ovens and griddles. Depending on laws in your area, you may also be required to work directly with a commissary (for more about commissaries see page 51) in which case it would be wise to also talk with them before proceeding. A commissary might be able to help you obtain a food truck or food cart that meets your needs and abides by all local regulations. A list of mobile food unit vendors is available in Appendix XII on page 161.

Food Carts

Food carts are smaller, more condensed, food service units that can be pushed on foot or pulled by a bike to move them from place to place. These carts come in all shapes and sizes, from small enough to breakdown and fit into your car to larger units that may be more stationary given their weight. Traditionally used for ice cream or hot dogs, today's food carts can come equipped with griddles, flat-top grills, and even a handwashing station if need be. The price for a food cart can start as low as $700-$1,000 for used carts and cost upwards of $5,000 or more if you opt for a newer version with all the bells and whistles. The more additional equipment you need, such as griddles, running water, refrigeration, and propane hookups, will obviously increase the cost. Carts can be as expensive as $20,000-$25,000 depending on what you need and how you plan on using it.

Food Trailers

Food trailers are another option and, since they don't contain an engine, are typically less expensive than food trucks. Not unlike food carts, food trailers can be as small as a compact trailer you hitch to a bike or as large as an Airstream trailer. Because trailers don't have an engine of their own, you want to make sure that the vehicle (or pedal power in the case of a food bike) is capable of pulling the food trailer before you buy it! Larger used food trailers typically start around $40,000 and can easily exceed $75,000 for new trailers depending on what functions you need it to serve.

Food Trucks

Food trucks, being fully mobile on their own without additional support, can sometimes be found used for as low as $10,000-$15,000, though used trucks in that price range are harder and harder to come by as more people open up food truck businesses. Realistically, you should plan to budget approximately $50,000 - $60,000 for a used truck that doesn't require any retrofitting. This means that you need to understand exactly what equipment you need for your food business before you start looking for a used food truck. If you have the means to purchase a new truck, they will cost – fully retrofitted and wrapped with your brand – upwards of $100,000 or more. This is certainly no small amount but it is significantly less than opening up a restaurant. Plus, unlike a restaurant, if you aren't attracting customers in one location you can simply turn the key and move your business to a new location!

Food Trucks & Gas Prices

One of the most important things anyone purchasing a food truck needs to understand is how many miles per gallon their food truck will get and what impact gas prices will have on your pocketbook. Gas prices are climbing and the higher they go the more that will eat into food truck entrepreneurs' bottom lines. The following example shows how much gas prices can affect your business. While the example uses generic figures, you can easily change these to fit your circumstance while using the same formula to see the direct impact on your food truck business. A gas price worksheet is available on page 156.

Assumptions for Food Truck X:

- Has a 20-gallon gas tank that requires diesel;
- Gets 10 miles per gallon;
- Drives approximately 50 miles daily to different selling locations;
- Works 25 days per month.

In March 2011 average gas prices were $3.87 per gallon which means that it would cost you $483.76 for gas over the course of the month. The math is below:

- $3.87 (cost per gallon) / 10 (miles per gallon) = $.39 (gas cost per mile)
- $.39 x 50 (miles driven per day) = $19.35 (gas cost per day)
- $19.35 x 25 (days worked per month) = $483.75

Food Trucks & Gas Prices

OK, you say, you can build that into your business plan and work with it. What happens, though, if gas prices go up further from there? For example, in March 2010 the average diesel gas price was $2.90 per gallon according to the U.S. Energy Information Administration. That means that if you had a food truck business in 2010, based on the above assumptions, you were spending $362.50 per month on gas and a year later are spending an additional $121.25 per month or an additional $1,455.00 per year on gas to get your truck in front of your hungry audience.

Since small food businesses can't hedge gas prices on the global market like many Fortune 500 companies, there are a few things food truck entrepreneurs can do to prevent gas costs from eating all of your profits:

- *Do the math and understand exactly how much you're spending per month on gas. The prices above were the nationwide average at that time but there is huge variability from region to region, so use the formula above and plug in the appropriate numbers for your business and locality. Then play with the numbers to understand how changes in gas prices one way or another affect your bottom line. What will happen to your business if gas prices rise $.25, $.50, or even $1+ per gallon?*

- *If you understand how price increases will impact your margins you can develop a backup plan that may include raising your food prices or limiting the miles driven per day. Obviously doing either of those may result in a loss of customers so you want to weigh the pros and cons carefully. However, if you know in advance that if gas prices raise a specific amount you will need to institute Plan B then you can quickly react to prices rather than going a month or more after gas prices increase before you realize you need to make changes.*

- *Find the lowest price gas you can. GasBuddy (www.gasbuddy.com) can help you locate the gas stations in your area that have the highest and lowest prices. You may want reroute your truck to stop by one of the lower-priced stations if you're trying to minimize your gas costs.*

Equipment Needs

While you don't want to spend more than you have to on equipment, one thing to keep in mind is that your menu may change in the future and you want to have the flexibility to make those changes. If, for example, your county allows you to cook food on the food truck and you're planning on selling freshly-cut pommes frites (fancy French fries) then you'd obviously need a fryer. However, you may one day decide it makes sense to add gourmet hamburgers to your menu, too and that's impossible unless you have a griddle. (Or you could always decide to deep fry the hamburgers and start a new fad!) You obviously don't want to stock a food truck or food trailer with every possible piece of equipment "just in case," but don't rule out a mobile food unit that has additional equipment if it works within your budget. And if you're planning to get a new mobile food unit you should ask about how much additional equipment costs, especially if you think you may one day expand your menu.

While much of the focus may be on what equipment is inside the mobile unit, you want to make sure that you also have the ability to easily serve people. It may sound simple but don't forget to make sure that you have a service window or two that you can easily access to take and deliver orders. This space should have a small counter for you to write down orders, if needed, and count out cash or run credit cards. Ideally, you also want this window positioned so that you can easily reach out to the customer, who will be on ground level, and take their money or give them their order. The last thing you or your back wants is to spend hours every day bent over so you can communicate with your customers. So when you're looking at your food truck or food trailer make sure you not only check out the equipment inside the unit but also view it from the customer's side and take into account how you would interact with them.

New vs. Used vs. Leasing vs. Buying

As mentioned earlier, it's possible to find used food carts, food trailers, and food trucks. The benefit to used, of course, is that they're typically much cheaper than buying a brand new unit. However, it's buyer-beware when it comes to purchasing a used unit and you should be sure to do your due diligence before handing over any money. You should take note of the condition the mobile food unit is in, check the wear and tear, inventory the equipment and make sure all equipment is working. Any equipment that isn't working or any mechanical problems you encounter in the mobile unit should be reflected in the price and you should consult with a repairman to determine how much it will cost you to get fixed. If you're buying a used food truck, be sure to have a mechanic check the engine and ensure that it's running smoothly.

While new mobile food units are usually more expensive, the beauty in buying new is the peace of mind that everything's working as it should. And if it's not, you will also likely have a warranty on the truck or cart. With a new food unit you also can customize the design and equipment. All of this comes with a price, but if you are committed to jumping into the mobile food business with two feet this may be the option for you.

Whether you're buying new or used, you should see if financing is available from the seller and how that impacts the overall financial picture of your business operations (more information about the financials is on page 95). If you go this route don't forget to take into account that your regularly-scheduled finance payments will include interest and you need to make sure you are comfortable paying this amount as outlined in the contract regardless of your sales in any given month.

Another alternative that may be available is leasing a food truck, food trailer, or food cart. The costs will vary widely and you will be restricted to existing mobile food units, which means you will likely have less ability to retrofit the unit unless you're willing to sign a long lease agreement. While the benefit of leasing is that it requires significantly less startup capital to get your business off the ground, you don't own the most critical component of your business – the mobile food unit itself. This may become a problem if you want to brand the food cart and are unable to or you spend money getting your leased food truck wrapped with your logo only to have to remove it when your lease runs out.

Overnight Parking

Before you get your mobile food unit you need to figure out where you're going to store it when it's not in operation. In certain parts of the country, food trucks are required by the health department to work with a commissary, which is a central site where food trucks can do all of their food preparation, park overnight and clean their units (more information about commissaries begins on page 51). If you don't live in one of those cities, then you need to figure out what parking options are available to you. For food carts, food bikes, and other smaller units the answer may be as easy as parking at your kitchen facility or even in your own garage. A food truck or larger food trailer is a little harder to fit in a normal-sized garage, and residential parking laws may prohibit you from parking a commercial vehicle on the street or in your driveway. In this case, you could consider renting a parking space in a parking lot. If you do, look for a secure or attended parking lot. The last thing you want is to show up at the food truck one morning to find that someone hosted a party in your truck while you were sleeping (and didn't clean up!).

Finding Your Kitchen On Wheels

Once you've determined what you need, the most obvious question is how to actually find and buy your food truck, food cart, or food trailer. Once again, it all depends on what you're looking for. If you're searching for used units it's worth checking out eBay (www.ebay.com) and your local Craigslist listings (www.craigslist.com) to see what, if anything, is available. Also, if you live in an area where mobile food businesses are required to work with commissaries, the commissaries themselves may be able to point you in the direction of someone who is selling a used unit or make suggestions about the best manufacturers if you want to purchase new. A short list of manufacturers and resellers is available in Appendix XII on page 161 but when in doubt you can easily do an Internet search to see if there are any additional vendors in your area.

Wrap It

Vehicle wraps are what transforms plain white food trucks or food carts into vibrant branded units that people recognize wherever they go. These wraps are made from a vinyl material that is safe for the vehicle and are printed with your custom design. In addition to making your mobile unit stand out and easy to find by customers, vehicle wraps offer some of the best advertising you will ever get. Even if you're just driving to the gas station to fill up, a wrapped food truck is advertising to everyone along the way! Most wrapping is done locally unless the manufacturer you buy a new unit from has an in-house graphics team. For this reason the easiest way to find a company that can wrap your food truck or food cart is to do an Internet search for businesses in your area that perform vehicle wraps. Prices vary widely depending on the size and shape of your mobile business and the complexity of your design.

If you plan on wrapping your food truck or food cart, take a moment to think about what information you want to quickly and easily convey to anyone who sees it. Obviously you want people to see your business name and logo and, if it's not easily discerned from the name, what it is your food truck actually sells. It may also be worthwhile to add your website, phone number, Twitter handle, and/or Facebook page to the wrap so that people know where to go to learn more about your company.

Mobile Food Permits

In addition to all the other business licenses necessary to start any new company (see page 45 for information about business licenses), most cities require that food trucks, food trailers, and food carts be inspected by the health department before you start operating and some cities will require that you also apply for a mobile food permit. In some places, like New York City, the number of permits given out each year is limited and the wait list is long.

If you are going to be cooking or baking on the truck, when the health department comes to inspect your mobile food unit they will want to test all of your refrigeration to ensure that you are storing foods at the correct temperatures. They may even temperature-test any food you're cooking to determine whether you are serving food that has been heated enough to kill any bacteria. You also will be required to maintain standards of cleanliness. It may all sound daunting but the end goal is to make sure that all food served from your truck is safe for public consumption and minimizes the risk of food-borne illnesses. While many people dread a visit from the health department, it's far better to work with them and limit your risks rather than get a visit from a lawyer hired by a sickened customer! Working with your local health department to make your mobile food business as clean and safe as possible just makes good business sense.

Insurance & Maintenance

Depending on what type of mobile food unit you've leased or purchased, you will want to let your business insurer know so that the unit is covered under any business liability insurance you purchase. In the case of mobile food you also should ask whether you need to purchase any additional vehicle insurance and make sure that it covers you and anyone else who will be driving the truck.

Don't forget that just like a car, food trucks, food trailers, and food carts need regularly-scheduled maintenance. In addition to keeping them spotlessly clean, not unlike a restaurant, you also need to be prepared to refill any propane tanks, deal with appliances that may break down, get the oil changed in food trucks, and make sure that all the tires are properly inflated. While none of these are overly expensive or time-consuming, they are pieces of owning a mobile food business that you should be aware of and build into your financial and time projections in advance. There's nothing more frustrating than waking up one morning to realize you have a flat tire. It's even more frustrating though when said flat tire is preventing you from getting out there and making money!

Even after your recipes have been perfected and you know where and how you are going to get your food truck or food cart, there are a number of licensing and permitting items you'll need to address before you can open for business. This section highlights some of the laws that govern how to start a mobile food business. Please note that this section covers the overarching business licensing rules but be aware that every state and city may have slightly different requirements. This book tries to provide a guideline of what you may encounter when setting up your business, but it's best to consult with an attorney or small business administration official with any questions about what exactly is required in your specific location.

Getting Started Tip

The Small Business Administration has one of the most comprehensive websites (www.sba.gov) about what is legally required to start a business. The site highlights exactly what forms are required by your state and local authorities based on your zip code. This book also has a list of business and health code licensing websites divided by state starting on page 165.

Registering Your Business

When starting your business there are four main steps you'll need to follow in order to get your business registered with the appropriate parties:

Deciding On Your Business Format

In the U.S. there are several ways the government classifies businesses. The choice is mainly yours to make, but it will impact everything from the taxes your business will owe to the level of personal financial risk you face in starting the business. The complexities and tax implications behind the differing business structures cannot be adequately described in detail here so you should talk to your local small business administration office or consult with a lawyer before making a final decision.

- Sole Proprietorship - A sole proprietorship is one of the easiest business structures to set up. In this structure, a single owner and the business are considered one and the same in the eyes of the law. Aside from minimal paperwork necessary to set up this business structure, one of the biggest benefits of sole proprietorship is that the business' profits and losses are reported directly onto the owner's personal tax forms. The biggest downside however is that your personal finances, including your home or other assets, may be at risk if the business can't pay its debts or is named in a legal matter.

- Partnership - Similar to a sole proprietorship except with two or more people. In a partnership, each partner shares in the risks and rewards of the business based on their percentage ownership interest. A partnership also is easy and inexpensive to setup, and the partners report their respective share of the business' profits and losses on their personal taxes. However, just like a sole proprietorship, partners also can be held personally liable for any debts, losses, or court judgments.

- Limited Liability Company (LLC) – A Limited Liability Company, also known as an LLC, is a hybrid business structure that gives business owners the relative ease and flexibility of a partnership with the personal liability protection of a corporation. In an LLC, the business' profits and losses flow through to the members (owners are called members in an LLC) and can be divided according to each member's percentage of ownership in the company. While LLCs are slightly more complex to setup then partnerships, the fact that LLCs protect the members personally from business debts and lawsuits is an important consideration. Setting up your business as an LLC is now an option in every state although each state does have slightly different requirements as to whether you need to draft and file Articles of Organization and/or an Operating Agreement. Since laws are different in each state, you should be sure to understand exactly what is required in your state before proceeding to set your business up as an LLC.

- Subchapter S Corporation - Subchapter S Corporations, also commonly known as Sub S or S Corporations, are a specific type of corporate business structure that mainly governs the disbursement of business profits and losses to the shareholders (owners are called shareholders in Subchapter S Corporations). Anyone considering classifying their business as a Subchapter S Corporation should definitely consult an attorney to help them through the many rules governing this type of business structure. At a very high level, profits and losses from a Subchapter S Corporation flow to the shareholders who then report it on their personal taxes. This means that the business is taxed only once – on an individual shareholder level – rather than being taxed at both the corporate and on an individual level.

However, your business has to meet several criteria; for example, all shareholders must be U.S. citizens to be eligible to be a Subchapter S Corporation. Another thing to note, which may be of concern to a mobile food business just starting out, is that all employees of a Subchapter S Corporation – including a shareholder who also works as an employee – must be paid a "reasonable wage" for their work. This means that if you plan on working in the business – i.e., taking care of administrative tasks, working in the kitchen, or serving from the truck - and you want your company to be registered as a Subchapter S then you will then need to include yourself on the company's payroll. While paying yourself a "reasonable wage" is a wonderful concept, when you're just starting out and are concerned about the cash flow of your business, the drawing of your own salary and the paying of employment taxes out of that cash flow may not make this business structure your best option.

- Subchapter C Corporation - Also known as C Corps or Chapter Cs, this business structure faces much more stringent government oversight and regulatory requirements. Anyone considering starting up a Subchapter C Corporation should consult an experienced attorney as the rules surrounding this business structure go far beyond what can adequately be covered here. In brief, the taxation rules around Subchapter C Corporations are such that any profits and losses are taxed on both a corporate level (paid by the business) and then again at the individual level as each shareholder must pay tax on the money they earn from the company.

Changing Business Structures

Many small, independently run businesses initially register as sole proprietorships, partnerships, or LLCs. These are generally much simpler business formats and require less tax preparation. While you should give considerable thought to your initial business structure, the good news is that, with few exceptions, you can change your business structure down the road if you decide it's necessary or if your business grows in such a way that it would be beneficial.

Regardless, how you structure your business impacts everything from what taxes you and your business need to pay, to laws governing how your business must operate, and can impact your financing options. As such, it is recommended that you speak with an attorney, small business administration representative, or other knowledgeable resource for guidance should you have any questions or concerns about the right business structure for your company.

Registering Your Business Name

Depending on your state and business structure, the name you register your company under may be as simple as your own personal name, the names of the partners, or a fictitious 'trade' name such as Joe's Baloney. Each state has a separate set of rules and may require that a name be registered with your state's Secretary of State and/or Department of Licensing. While it may sound complicated, don't be deterred. Every state has a website that explains their specific steps and in most cases, you should be able to complete the entire process online. More information, outlined by state, is available in Appendix XV on page 165.

Naming Your Business Tip

If you are registering a trade name for the business, keep in mind not just where the company is today but where you might like it to go in the future and avoid using a name that will lock you into one niche market. For example, rather than registering your company under the trade name "Scrumptious Cookies," register it as 'Scrumptious Baked Goods' or simply 'Scrumptious.' Even if you currently plan to offer only cookies, you will have the flexibility to grow into other areas such as croissants and cakes down the road. Give yourself room to grow with a name that can grow with you.

Trademarking Your Business Name

You certainly don't need to trademark your business name, but it is worthwhile to look into the process and decide if you have the time and money to invest into trademarking the name you will use in any marketing, advertising, and packaging. Obtaining a trademark for your business name will protect a competitor from using a similar business name that may cause confusion among your customers. As an example,

Greta's Gluten-Free Goodies wouldn't want a competitor to come into the same market with the name Gertle's Gluten-Free Goodies. The similarities between the two could easily cause confusion and Greta's customers may mistakenly buy Gertle's products, resulting in a loss of revenue for Greta. By filing a trademark for the name Greta's Gluten-Free Goodies, Greta could take action against Gertle in this instance and, if the Patent and Trademark Office ruled in Greta's favor, could force Gertle to change their business name. More information about trademarking your business name, logo, or other distinguishing mark can be found at the U.S. Patent and Trademark Office's website (www.uspto.gov) or by consulting an experienced trademark attorney.

Obtaining Your Employer Identification Number

Even if you don't plan to hire employees, depending on your business structure, you may need to register your business with the Internal Revenue Service and obtain your Employer Identification Number (commonly referred to as an EIN). The IRS website (www.irs.gov) has a comprehensive guide outlining who needs EINs and how to obtain them along with an online EIN application.

Register with Your State, County, and City

Depending on your local regulations, you may be required to register your business with your state and local tax authorities. During this step you will be given information about how to apply for a reseller certificate if it is required in your state. This certifies that you are a recognized business in your state and enables you to avoid paying sales tax on many of the ingredients you'll be buying for your business as long as the ingredients are going into products that will be sold to the public. As with other registration paperwork, most if not all of the state and local-level registration forms are available online in conjunction with extensive information about other requirements specific to your area.

Liability Insurance

While not always required by the state or federal government, it's a good idea to get liability insurance for your company that protects against loss of sales or property in the event of a catastrophe and protects the business financially from lawsuits. Given how litigious our society has become, liability insurance provides you and your business with an added layer of protection from any legal issues that may arise. This is especially important in the case of businesses that are structured as sole proprietorships or partnerships where lawsuits could impact both your business and personal finances. Many larger, well-respected insurance companies offer small business liability insurance, so ask your personal insurance agent for quotes or for references to other insurance companies who work with small businesses. While it can be an added expense when starting up the business, for a few hundred dollars a year, liability insurance can provide you with $1,000,000 or more of liability coverage and the comfort that your business and your personal finances will be safe should someone file a lawsuit against your company.

Commissaries vs. Kitchens

As mentioned earlier, some municipalities require that mobile food businesses work with commissaries to legally operate in that area. Because this is such a large piece of the mobile food business puzzle, you should consult with your local health department to understand what rules apply to your location. A brief description of commissaries and commercial kitchen options is below.

Commissaries

Some states require the mobile food vendors use a commissary which are registered and secure locations where you store your food truck or food cart overnight. Commissaries also typically provide your unit with clean water necessary for operating your business and you may be required to purchase some or all of your wholesale ingredients through them. Depending on the set up of the commissary and the laws in your area, you also may have access to refrigeration, dry storage, and an area for food preparation. Commissaries can cost a few hundred dollars a month or, if you live in an expensive city, to more than $1,000 per month regardless of how often you take out your truck.

Obviously this is a significant fixed operating cost, but commissaries also can be a huge source of information for you; they understand what is required to operate in your specific area and will be able to help guide you through some of the legalities of starting up your food truck business. They also may be able to point you in the direction of a good local source to purchase or lease your food truck, food trailer, or food cart. Given that they can be such a wealth of local knowledge, it's worthwhile to develop a solid relationship with your commissary managers (hint – paying your rent on time each month is a great start!).

Kitchens

If you live in a city that doesn't require you work from a commissary, you will still need some place for food preparation and food storage during the off-hours. Unless you have a burning desire to spend $100,000 on renting a location and building it out into a commercial kitchen, in most cases the best option for mobile food entrepreneurs is to rent or lease commercial kitchen space. A few commercial kitchen space options follow on the next pages but before you sign on the dotted line make sure that the space meets local health department standards. You may want to have your health department come by and check out the space if you have any questions or concerns. The last thing you want is to sign a lease only to realize that the kitchen doesn't, say, have the required three-basin sink that is needed before the health department will issue an operating permit.

Shared Commercial Kitchen Space/Kitchen Incubator

In the past few years a new concept of "shared" kitchen space, also known as kitchen incubators, has popped up. Found mostly in larger cities, the idea is that one individual or investor rents or owns the commercial kitchen space and then subleases the space to several food entrepreneurs on an hourly or monthly basis. This means you only have to pay for the time you anticipate using, which is significantly cheaper then leasing an entire commercial kitchen on your own. In many cases the shared kitchens will require you to schedule your hours in advance to ensure there aren't time conflicts with other food entrepreneurs. To find a shared commercial kitchen or kitchen incubator in your area, you can check Commercial Kitchen For Rent (www.commercialkitchenforrent.com) for a list of commercial kitchens broken out by state or check the commercial rental section of Craigslist or another community forum.

Extra Time In A Neighborhood Restaurant Or Bakery

Bakeries and restaurants that already have kitchen space may only use it certain hours during the day, but they are still paying rent for a full 24 hours every day. Consider approaching one of these establishments to see whether they'd be willing to rent any of their "off" time to your mobile food business. Of course, keep your schedule in mind before talking to specific food businesses. For example, if you plan on running a gourmet food truck that serves lunch to business people and would need to do your prep work first thing in the morning then it would be a waste of time to approach a local bakery that also is fully staffed in the morning to bake all their bread.

Community Kitchen Space

The easiest solution may be a community kitchen space such as at a church, synagogue, or other community association that puts on events or feeds large numbers of people. If these kitchens are only used sporadically or only used on specific days of the week, they may be willing to rent out time to you as an additional revenue source. Take stock of the equipment they have to make sure it includes everything you need and be sure to take into consideration any limitations this type of space may put on you. For example, if your business plan includes prepping on the weekends, a church's kitchen – which is typically busy on Saturdays and Sundays – may be occupied on the days you'd need it most. Along those same lines, a synagogue may not allow your mobile food business to prepare meat in their kitchen due to dietary restrictions of their congregation.

Home-based Kitchens

Some states currently allow for food preparation in the comfort of your own kitchen. Loosely known as Cottage Food Laws, there is a movement across the U.S. to allow home-based food businesses to be licensed and able to sell their products to the public. Whether this means you will be able to use your home kitchen as the base for your mobile food business, though, depends on where you live.

While each state differs, in most cases the states that do allow for home-based food businesses only allow for production of food that isn't potentially hazardous, such as baked goods that don't require certain storage temperatures, pickled products, jams, jellies, and other items such as granola, and candy. Because every state is different in what they allow from home-based food businesses, it is critical that you read the fine print for your state. Even in states that have passed cottage food laws, some states still require that your home kitchen be licensed by a health department official while others let you operate out of your kitchen without any oversight. Some won't allow kids or pets in a home kitchen you use for your business, which is not feasible if you only have one kitchen and have kids or pets in your home (and plan on keeping them!). Some limit where you can sell your products and others put limits on how much revenue your business can make in a year which, after you take your costs into account, may not make it a profitable venture for you. Again, it's critical that you talk with your local health department to understand if this is an option for your food truck, food trailer, or food cart business.

Other Health Code Considerations

In addition to the health department inspection for your mobile unit and kitchen spaces, most municipalities require that anyone who will be working with food or serving food to the public needs to have a food handler's certificate. The idea that you have to find time in your busy schedule to take a safe food handling course probably made you groan, right? Don't worry, most courses are only a few hours long and if you simply pay attention during the class and read the material they provide to you, the final test should be no problem. The benefit of this course is that it helps you and everyone who may work with you understand the risk of food-borne illness and how bacteria is spread through unsafe food handling. On the off chance that the thought of making your customers ill isn't enough to motivate you, then be aware that the health inspector may come by at any point to spot-check your business and may ask to see food handler certificates for anyone working. Contact your local health department for more information and, if necessary, specific class schedules.

One of the most obvious benefits of a mobile food business is that it *is* mobile and you are not tied to one specific spot day in and day out. Not only are a range of location options available to you though, there are numerous ways you can make money with your food truck, food trailer, or food cart.

Cash vs. Credit/Debit Cards

Before you start selling your food you should determine whether you're going to only accept cash for orders or if you also will take debit and credit cards. The beauty of only taking cash is that you don't have to set up a merchant account to accept credit cards and you won't lose a percentage of each sale to the merchant account fee. While it is certainly possible and easier to deal with a cash-only system, you run the risk of turning away customers who don't carry cash on them at all times. Do you really want a hungry customer to walk away to a competitor that does accept credit and debit cards? Not to mention that when you only accept cash you will need to make sure you have a significant amount of money available on the truck everyday to make change.

If you decide to, in addition to cash, also accept debit and credit cards, you will need to get a merchant account set up for your business. A merchant account essentially acts as the go-between from your business to the customer's credit card company. In a nutshell, when a customer buys an item and pays for it with a credit or debit card, the business charges the card, which alerts the merchant account. The merchant account acts as an intermediary and credits the money to the business' account and then works with the credit card issuing company to, essentially, get reimbursed. You will need a credit card terminal for your food truck or food cart. This is a physical credit card processing machine that you use to run the customer's card.

All merchant account companies charge fees for using their services, which may include a monthly fee for the credit card terminal, a set charge per transaction and a percentage of the sale price. Some of these fees go straight to the merchant account while others are passed onto the specific credit card issuing companies themselves. These fees can start to add up quickly so shop around for the best rates and the best combination of services. An easy place to begin your search is with companies like PayPal (www.paypal.com) or Costco (www.costco.com) that both offer merchant account services to small businesses. Quicken (www.quicken.intuit.com) and QuickBooks (www.quickbooks.intuit.com) also have merchant account services available for those who use their accounting software programs. Don't forget that this is your business revenue so be sure you understand and are comfortable with all the terms of the merchant account you choose.

Credit Card Processing Goes Mobile

One innovative option for credit card payment for mobile businesses on the go is Square®. Compatible with iPad, iPhone, and Android devices, Square is an attachment you add to your mobile unit of choice that enables small businesses to accept Visa, Mastercard, American Express, and Discover cards without an expensive merchant account or credit card processing terminal. With low per transaction fees, fast setup, next-day payment to the bank account of your choice, and no monthly fees, Square is poised to revolutionize the merchant account world for small businesses. Just remember, that Square needs wireless access in order to process cards! More information about Square can be found at https://squareup.com/.

Street Sales

If you've been thinking about getting a food truck, food trailer, or food cart then you probably envision yourself selling your food on crowded street corners. This is the image most people associate with mobile food businesses for good reason. Parking on the street is a fast and easy way to get your business seen by passers-by and it's possible to stay for a few hours before moving on to a new location. However, this doesn't mean you can just roll up to any street corner and start selling.

The first thing you need to do is make a list of locations where you'd like to park your mobile unit and sell. This, like so many of the other big decisions when it comes to your business, depends on who your target audience is. Pull out the Competitive Analysis you created in Chapter 3 to use as your guide through this process.

With knowledge about who your target audience is, the next step is to figure out where they congregate. At a high level this shouldn't be too hard. In the Sweet Bits Treat Truck example, the focus is on children and families so it makes sense to plan on taking the truck to beaches, parks, children's sporting events, festivals and farmers' markets – all places where children and families might spend time. It gets a little more complex when you decide to figure out where exactly, i.e. the corner of 5th and Vine or 4th and Market, you'll be stopping. As with all things real estate, the key is location, location, location.

The best way to find those prime locations is to spend some time scouting the areas you highlighted as popular for your target audience. Make note of where people are and what they're doing as well as what competitors – other mobile units and brick-and-mortar restaurants – are nearby. You want know if it's better to park on the corner of 2nd Street as opposed to 3rd Street because there's more foot traffic at the former. Or perhaps you think that parking your food truck or food cart near a courthouse is a good idea until your research reveals that everyone around the court house is running around for court cases and grab their lunch from a surprising competitor — the court cafeteria. Doing actual in-person scouting will help you learn more about the area and more about the behaviors of your target market. From this you'll be able to compile a list of top parking locations.

Your next step will be to figure out what the parking laws are for those prime locations to see if you can even set up shop there. Every city and state has different parking rules when it comes to mobile food businesses. In some cases you may be able to secure a business owner's permission to park in their private parking lot without incurring a fee. In other cases, if you want to park on the street you may need to feed the meter. Or you may be prohibited from parking on the street entirely if the city doesn't allow food trucks on city streets or if laws have been passed that prevent you from being within a certain distance of a brick-and-mortar food establishment. Even if you can park on the street, some cities limit the amount of time they'll allow you to park there before requiring you to move on. Meanwhile in other cities, you can stay parked in one spot all day if you choose as long as you have permission from a nearby establishment to use their bathroom and keep feeding the meter. It's imperative that you understand the parking rules for each neighborhood you plan on visiting otherwise parking tickets can start to quickly eat away at your profits. Not to mention that the last thing you want customers to see is several policemen coming up to your food truck unless it's to grab a bite to eat themselves!

Some towns and cities that don't allow mobile food businesses on city streets are now bowing to public pressure and creating food truck stops where all the area food trucks, food trailers, and food carts can congregate for either one night a week or month or on a daily basis. While this may not give you the mobility you were hoping for, these types of events do draw large crowds who are eager for variety, so don't rule them out entirely.

Once you determine the best locations to reach your target customers and have worked out any parking legalities, it's worthwhile to set up a regular schedule so that people know when and where to expect you. This doesn't mean you have to stay static; the point of a mobile food business is the flexibility it gives you to move around. You may decide to park your truck in a different place for lunch every day but the key is to keep the schedule consistent. That way, people learn that every Monday you'll be at the corner of 3rd and Main, every Tuesday you'll be parked next to the car dealership on Maple, and so on. This consistency will help your business grow. You need to give people time to hear about you, find you, try your food, and then tell their friends about your business and this likely won't all happen overnight. Stick with your schedule for a few weeks and see if your sales are growing as the word gets out. If not, it may be time to switch locations and try something new. Or, before you know it, you may just find you've got a line down the street.

Catering and Private Events

Because food trucks, food trailers, and food carts can so easily be moved, more and more mobile food businesses are offering their services for private events. You can take your gourmet taco truck to a Mexican-themed wedding or drive your organic popsicle truck to a corporate campus on a hot summer afternoon. The benefit of these contracted events is that you will get paid regardless of what the weather is like, which is what usually has the biggest impact on retail street sales. Catering and private events also are a great way to add to your sales on slower days or even during certain times of the year when business is slow. While you always need to weigh the pros and cons of accepting any contract that would take you away from your normal routine, if you get asked to work at an event during a time when your

[61]

food business is normally not on the road – or during a time that is historically slow – that's supplemental revenue!

To attract private events, you should include catering information on your website and any other marketing material you have. Depending on how much of your energy you want to focus on private events you can also look to place private event specific ads on Facebook or in magazines (additional Marketing techniques are explained in-depth beginning on page 69). Another option is to contact area party planners and the human resources department of local companies. Don't forget that it's always wise to have information about your catering services with you at all times; you never know if the next person who comes up to your food truck window on the street may be planning a giant retirement bash for their CEO!

Should you be approached for a wedding or other personal private event, you need to work out with the planner how much you will be paid. Depending on what it is you sell, you may want to determine an upfront cost that will cover any and all product you give away to guests. Alternatively you may decide to charge an hourly fee and then a reduced 'per piece' price. In this case, you would need to keep track of how much product you give away during the event to charge the party planner accordingly afterwards.

Corporate events typically work a little differently. In some cases you may be invited onto the corporate campus to sell your food, but it's the responsibility of the employees to pay you. If it's a big enough firm or corporate campus, you may not want to ask for an hourly fee since your truck or cart will be in front of their employees, all of whom are potential customers. You can always ask though that a company-wide email be sent out alerting employees to your presence on ground to help draw traffic your way.

Sometimes, though, corporations like to reward their employees by giving away free food as a little perk. For example, a company may contact you about providing your organic artisan ice cream to employees on a hot Friday afternoon. In this case you would want to work out in advance how much ice cream you plan on giving away so that you can include your time and product cost in the estimate you provide to the human resources department. The other option, just like private personal events, is to keep track of how many units you give away and charge the company for that amount.

In either case, you want to work closely with the corporation's planner or organizer to make sure both of you fully understand what is expected. Are you supposed to offer your full food truck menu to guests or only have a select number of choices available (and if so, does the planner have preferences as to which menu items)? Is a deposit required to secure your services (highly recommended) and how long after the event will you get paid? What time are you expected to be there and how long are you expected to stay? Make sure that all of this is laid out in a contract that is signed by both parties so there are no misunderstandings.

Farmers' Markets, Festivals & Fairs

Farmers' markets, festivals, and fairs are a great way to get your mobile food business in front of large groups of people in one easy shot. These events are usually marketed well in advance and once at the event, visitors don't want to have to leave to find food. These events can either supplement your regular street income or, depending on the focus of your mobile food business, it is possible to do very well by only attending key farmers' markets or festivals throughout the year. In fact there are some mobile food vendors who make so much money by working state fairs that they only have to work a few months a year!

It's important to note that you can't simply roll up to one of these events and expect to be given space. In almost every case you must apply in advance to be accepted into the event, which requires you to keep an eye on the calendar and make sure you get the event application turned in before the deadline. Unfortunately, not every venue allows food vendors so be sure to read the application rules thoroughly before applying. The application rules also should stipulate whether you are required to have a separate food vending permit as is required in some municipalities.

The costs associated with selling at these types of events vary widely but it should be clearly stated in the application you submit. In many cases you will be required to pay a flat booth fee that could range from $10 for a farmers' market to a few hundred or even several thousand dollars for larger events. In some cases you may be required to pay a percentage of your sales to the event organizers. Before you submit your application, you need to determine whether you can sell enough food to cover your event costs and still make enough money to make it worthwhile. It's useful to look at past event vendors to determine if any of your direct competitors might be there. If it looks like there are going to be three pulled-pork mobile vendors at an event that only draws 2,000 people then you have to seriously ask yourself whether adding your pulled-pork truck to the mix will be a good use of your time.

Sporting Events

Situated just outside Seattle's Qwest Field before every Seattle Sounders professional soccer game are two food trucks that have endless lines in the hours before the games begin. Sporting events, be it professional, amateur, or collegiate, draw people who all need to eat at one point or another. Because sporting venues often have with onsite concessionaires, ask the sporting venue directly to determine if you can park your food truck on their property.

If you can't get permission to park on their property, that doesn't mean you have to abandon the idea of feeding the hungry sporting masses. Take a look at the routes people use to get to the game and find a way to place your food truck in their path. For example, if most people are taking public transportation to the game is there a place you can legally park near the bus or subway stop so that that people pass right by you on the way to or from the game? Perhaps you know fans congregate in a specific part of the city before or after the game and it might be possible to bring your food business to them there.

Wholesale Accounts

Let's say your food cart business really takes off. Your strong following may in turn may capture the attention of stores that want to carry your products. For some food businesses, the transition can be easy. Items like cookies or ice cream that can be easily packaged for sale in a retail store. Other items, though, like your famous grilled cheese sandwiches, are harder to sell wholesale. That doesn't mean wholesale is impossible, it just means you have to think outside the box a little more. While selling your grilled cheese in stores isn't an option, you could consider bottling some of the popular handmade spicy ketchup you serve with your sandwiches and sell that wholesale instead.

Wholesale accounts are unique. First and foremost, wholesale accounts will require that you provide them with a lower per-unit cost so they can mark the product up to sell to their customers. You need to determine what your product costs are, including any packaging costs you may incur (see page 95 for more information about product cost), and then determine how much you will charge for wholesale accounts. While you may not make as much per unit with wholesale accounts, you can stipulate that the store take a minimum number of units, for example you can require that they order your spicy ketchup in case packs of 24, to make it worth your while.

Before you enter into any wholesale contract you should also ask several key questions:

- How are you getting paid? As long as the retailer is credit worthy, checks are the easiest method of payment and you won't have credit card processing fees taken out of the payment you receive. However, it's always advisable that you have retailers' credit card numbers so that you can charge their card if they don't pay on time.

- When are you getting paid? Any contract you sign or purchase order you receive should describe when you will be paid – either on delivery, Net 15 (15 days after you ship or deliver the order), Net 30 (30 days after you ship or deliver the order), etc.

- Can they return unsold items to you? It should be outlined in the contract or purchase order if retailers can return unsold product to you after a certain period of time.

Don't forget that you should also brand any packaging you use for your wholesale accounts. Part of the reason these stores are interested in you is because your food truck or food cart is associated with a superior product. You want to make it easy for shoppers to recognize your product on store shelves.

Online Retail

If you have a product you are selling wholesale, it may be worthwhile to see if you can sell this same product via online retail channels. It is possible to set up an ecommerce website that will enable you to take online orders from your web visitors. Another option is to try and get your product featured on Foodzie (www.foodzie.com) or other food-related online sites like Daily Gourmet (www.dailygourmet.com). These sites enable you to sell through their site and, if you don't have a web store set up on your own site, you can direct online customers to these sites to place orders. Keep in mind that if you choose to open up an online retail store you must have the time to ship any orders and must make sure that your product can be safely shipped without spoiling, breaking, or otherwise compromising the quality of the item.

Home Delivery

Though the goal of most mobile food businesses is to get the customers to come to them, the fact that your business can be moved means you also can bring your business to customers. A food bike business with a trailer might be able to easily maneuver through neighborhoods delivering pre-ordered (via Twitter perhaps!) goodies, or if your popsicle business slows down significantly in the winter months, you may decide to offer home delivery for those customers wanting a taste of sunshine. While it's not a traditional business model for mobile food businesses, when done right, home delivery can help you bring in extra cash and keep your customers connected to you.

All that research you've done about who your target market is now comes into play. Understanding your customers, and what motivates them, enables you create a sales and marketing strategy that will speak to them and get them to head your way.

Branding

After spending all this time, energy, and money getting your mobile food business started, you want to make sure it's memorable and recognizable to your customers. You want your customers to tell their friends and that won't be accomplished if they can't remember the name of your business. Branding your company will help in this. One of the most famous examples of food branding is McDonald's® golden arches. No matter where in the world you go, that distinctive red and gold color lets you know exactly what you can expect to find inside. Obviously, branding makes the product recognizable, but it also conjures up in each customer memories of a personal experiences and feelings. In the above case, some may associate the golden arches with a delicious and inexpensive family meal. Others, however, may consider that the food is too greasy and salt-laden for their tastes.

Building a brand, which includes everything from your business name to your logo to any significant colors you use, will help people recognize your mobile food business. It's advisable to work with a graphic artist to help you create your brand since it will be, in most cases, the first impression your audience has of your company. For example, the wrap on your food truck should be eye-catching and inviting. It doesn't matter how good your food is if people won't come over to your truck or trailer to try it.

The prices for hiring a graphic artist can run the gamut depending on the artist's experience and if they're affiliated with a graphic design firm. If you don't know a graphic designer personally, you can search for a freelance graphic artist in your community by doing an internet search or through sites like www.ifreelance.com, www.graphicdesigners.freelancers.com and www.elance.com. A less expensive option is to approach your local college to see if any graphic design students might want to take the work on as they will likely charge you less than a professional graphic design firm. This was the route Nike®, the running shoe company, took in its early days when the management team hired a graphic design student to create a logo for them. The famous "swoosh" logo, which Nike has used for more than 30 years, cost them $35. Talk about getting an effective logo cheaply! Lest you fear the graphic artist was ripped off, when Nike went public they gave the graphic artist stock shares, which made her a significant amount of money.

While working with a graphic artist, you should clearly convey to them who your target market is so your branding is consistent with that audience. The brand your graphic artist creates for a food truck that's targeting college students and the late-night crowd will likely be quite different from the brand created for a food cart that will be setting up shop near playgrounds.

Make sure you're happy with the work the graphic artist does, and you should be willing to pay for their time to make changes as needed. You don't want to start your company with a brand image you're not happy with since the brand should extend to and remain consistent in all aspects of your marketing. It's worthwhile to spend the time and, if needed, the money to make sure that the brand image you launch your company with is the best possible graphic representation of your mobile food business.

Marketing Strategy

Traditionally, marketing focused on how you would get your message out to consumers. This typically revolved around shouting your message as loud as possible, usually in the form of an advertisement, promotion, or discount, in the hopes that your target market would hear it. Outbound marketing, as this is now known, is still a useful tool but today it's possible for food entrepreneurs to put a large part of their marketing budget and energies into making themselves more easily found by customers who are actively looking for them; a concept referred to as inbound marketing. To understand the difference, think of it this way: buying ad space in a magazine is outbound marketing whereas inbound marketing would include something like creating a blog about your artisan food company that can easily be found by web search engines so that anyone doing a web search for, say, organic bread in your city, would be directed to your site. In the first case, you put the ad out there in front of thousands of people in the hopes that the organic bread consumer will see it.   In the case of inbound marketing, you focus instead on getting your message to those who are actually looking for what you sell.

One benefit of inbound marketing for food entrepreneurs is that it is usually significantly cheaper than traditional outbound marketing. Whereas a magazine ad could easily cost thousands of dollars to run for just one month, you can create a Facebook fan page that customers can interact with and help drive traffic to your food truck or food trailer for free. That doesn't mean that outbound marketing techniques should be abandoned entirely. First and foremost, many inbound marketing tactics take significantly more time and energy to develop. As the Internet continues to rapidly change, you have to be ready to keep your message fresh for your audience and easily found by web search engines. This means that you might have to commit to posting regularly on social media tools like Facebook or Twitter or be ready to write multiple blog posts for readers to enjoy. For an already busy mobile business entrepreneur tasked with shopping for ingredients, preparing the product, driving the truck, selling food, and doing all the associated administrative work, this may be too much.

As with most important business decisions, the combination of marketing strategies you use will depend on who your audience is. If you hope to get your truck in front of technologically-savvy college students then a marketing strategy that is heavy on inbound marketing techniques like using social media might be the way to go. Alternatively, if you are looking to grow the catering side of your food truck business, then you may want to attend local wedding tradeshows or invest in local wedding magazine ads to better reach that market.

A description of several outbound and inbound marketing tools are listed on the following page. Keep in mind, though, that as the Internet continues to evolve, new marketing tools are being created daily.

Outbound Marketing

This is what people typically think of when you mention marketing. Outbound marketing focuses on talking to customers in the hopes that what you say or show them will be enough to drive them to your business. The main problem with this type of marketing, a problem marketers have long tried to deal with, is that it's hard to always make sure your customers actually hear your message. These days people are bombarded with so many messages that it's harder and harder to break through the clutter, which means your marketing dollars could be going to waste. This doesn't mean that outbound marketing doesn't have its place. With the advent of new technology, outbound marketing has become far more sophisticated and can help you effectively share information with your customers and potential customers.

Advertising

The famous phrase about advertising, attributed to Ogilvy advertising client John Wanamaker, goes something along the lines of "I know that half of my advertising dollars are wasted, I just don't know which half!" Most traditional advertising methods, such as print ads, radio ads, television ads, or outdoor ads like billboards or bus placards are extremely expensive for an artisan food company to use. Even if you do have the means, you need to weigh what this type of advertising will do for your business before investing the money. The hard part for a mobile food business is that if you want to advertise, you need to clearly send the message that you don't have a traditional brick-and-mortar location and that your location and hours may vary by day. Given that many traditional ads need to be submitted well in advance for publication or creation, these avenues may not be a best for a food business like yours that is more flexible and can change as situations dictate.

Internet ads, on the other hand, require less advance time to implement and better target to your desired demographic. Given that your food business will be focused on a very specific area, it may be worthwhile to buy banner ad or sponsor space on hyper-local neighborhood blogs. Another relatively inexpensive advertising option is pay-per-click advertising where you can control how much is spent in any one day or any one timeframe. With services like Google Adwords (www.google.com/adwords) and Facebook ads (www.facebook.com/ads) you can create ads that will be seen by a very specific audience and you only pay for those people who click on your ad for more information. More information about Facebook is available on page 84.

Don't forget that your food truck, food trailer, or food cart will also be a form of advertising in and of itself. Simply parking your food truck at a specific street corner or taking your food cart to a farmers' market will advertise your business to potential customers. Be sure to have business cards or other marketing material that you can hand out to customers if they'd like to take information with them. This is especially important if your food truck or food cart also offers corporate or special events catering. Should someone approach with a question about catering you want to be able to provide them with more information and answer any questions on the spot.

What About Daily Deal Sites?

In the "Great Recession," online daily deal sites took off with Groupon and Living Social leading the way. Essentially these sites work with small businesses to email deals, usually a minimum of 50 percent off, to their subscriber base. The benefit of these sites to food entrepreneurs is that these promotions can drive significant traffic at no upfront cost. However, in addition to offering a deep discount to be featured, businesses also must pay a percentage of the deal's sales to the daily deal site. This means that if a food truck offers $20 worth of food for $10 the daily deal site may take as much as 50% of the sale as their percentage so the food truck would only be making $5 on each sale but must provide $20 worth of food.

For businesses, such as food businesses, that incur a lot of variable costs associated with each sale, these daily deal sites need to be carefully considered before signing up. Though these sites may be a good way to bring in immediate revenue — since you are paid based on how many people purchase the deal and not how many people actually redeem the deal — you need to determine whether the amount you will be making off each sale is profitable to you given your costs.

You also need to consider the impact a daily deal will have on your brand and on your customers. If your deal is a success, it may lead to longer wait times at your food truck, which could upset new and returning customers. You'd hate for them to take their business elsewhere and share their negative experience with friends, on blogs, or on review sites like Yelp (www.yelp.com). The other big risk of daily deals is that it could start to train your customers to expect that you'll discount and make them unwilling pay full retail price for your food.

Prior to the advent of social media, e-newsletters – and before that, old-fashioned direct mail newsletters — were the way many small businesses kept in contact with their customers. Though e-newsletters may be losing ground to tools like Facebook and blog posts, there is still a place for this form of marketing. Even if your customers are social media-savvy, e-newsletters are a great way to provide your audience with more insight and information into your business. After all, it can be hard to share a lot of information in the 140-character limit on Twitter. A quarterly e-newsletter, on the other hand, gives you more space to delve into topics that are interesting to your audience and keep you connected to them. This is especially important for food trucks in locations that don't operate year-round due to weather. You don't want your customers to forget about you in the off season so sending engaging e-newsletters can help keep your company on the top of their minds.

This may sound obvious, but in order to send e-newsletters you need email addresses. If you don't yet have an existing email database you can work from, the easiest way to collect email addresses from your customers is to place an e-newsletter signup on your website or blog or encourage people on your Facebook or Twitter posts to add their names to the list. You also can collect email addresses at your truck or cart via a business card drop off or email signup list.

Two of the most commonly used e-newsletter services by small businesses as of the printing of this book are MailChimp (www.mailchimp.com) and Constant Contact (www.constantcontact.com). Both of these services enable you to easily and inexpensively create and send e-newsletters that fit your brand while remaining compliant with the laws of the CAN-SPAM Act. Additionally, both systems can track results for you so that you can determine how many people opened your e-newsletter, how many forwarded it on to a friend, and which links readers clicked on.

Promotion & Sponsorships

When it comes to promoting your business, the only limitation is your own imagination. If the market is right, you can consider purchasing sponsorships to certain events or, as mentioned earlier, sponsoring highly- localized blogs if it will help promote your brand and business. Also think about working with other businesses or other mobile food vendors to put together special events that will draw new customers, like a Friday night "Chowdown" street food feast featuring area food trucks or a "Gawk & Munch" combination art walk and food cart festival in partnership with local art galleries.

Inbound Marketing

In a nutshell, inbound marketing is a way for you to share information with people who actually want to hear what you have to say. Whereas outbound marketing talks *to* customers, inbound marketing enables you to build relationships and talk *with* your audience. In addition to helping you build a brand and engage your loyal customers, inbound marketing also makes it easier than ever for food carts, food trucks, and other mobile food businesses to update people on where you're currently located and where you might be moving to next.

Truth be told, this section was the last one to be written. Not because it isn't important, but because inbound marketing is so incredibly fluid that it likely will have changed by the time you're reading this. As the Internet continues to evolve, new inbound marketing tools are being created at lightning speed. A brief outline of some of the most popular inbound marketing tools is below but if you want to stay up-to-date on inbound marketing or need more information, be sure to check out HubSpot (www.hubspot.com), a marketing software company focused on small and medium-sized business. Their online resource center has a wealth of informative inbound marketing blog posts and webcasts available free of charge.

Your Website

Technically, your company website is considered inbound marketing because someone must either search specifically for your food business or search for a word referenced in your site to find the website itself. The great thing is that your site can market your company around the clock. Even when you're sleeping your website will tell late-night web searchers about your company.

There are three main ways you can get a website up and running. The easiest, but most expensive, is to contract with a web developer who will be able to get your website's domain name registered and get the site going with minimal hands-on work from you. In addition to taking this chore off your plate, one of the biggest benefits is that a good web designer will be able to create a site that is in-line with the brand you're creating for your company. Depending on how complex a site you want, a web developer may charge you anywhere from $1,500 to $10,000 or more for your site. Of course if you have a friend or family member, or know of a student with strong web skills, you may be able to get a break on the rate.

If you do decide to work with a web developer, it is worthwhile to do some research on your own first to determine what type of look and functionality you like in websites. This way you will not only be able to provide the designer with examples of work you like, but you may also be able to find your web developer this way! If you see a website you particularly like, check the bottom of the web page as the name of the developer or design company will often be included along with a link to their own website. It's an easy way to start getting in touch with web developers and learn more about what prices they charge.

Another easy and increasingly popular website option for small food businesses is to set up a website via a blog site like WordPress (www.wordpress.com) or Blogger (www.blogger.com). The upside to this is that these programs require little technological knowledge and you can quickly and easily update your own site, which is key for a mobile food business on the move. Plus these sites currently allow you to host your site with them free of charge.

If you go through a blog site, you will have two naming options for your website. You can either purchase a domain name (your website name) directly through the blog or you can use the website address they provide free of charge. If you go the latter route, you will have a web address along the lines of www.yourcompanyname.blogname.com. This can be a mouthful for people to remember, make it harder to find your site online, and in some people's mind make your business look less professional. For this reason, if you decide to use a blog site to create and update your website, it's recommended that you purchase a domain name of your own.

One thing that steers people away from blog sites as the main portal for their website is that it's believed you are somewhat constrained in your website functionality and you won't be able to incorporate online shopping carts or Flash graphics. While that used to be true, today's blogs can easily be customized by an experienced web developer or someone with web coding experience. So while you can create a free website via a blog site, if you want more functionality then the free options will allow it is possible to hire a web developer to redesign your blog-based site typically at less cost than a full website design from scratch. More information about blogs starts on page 83.

If you don't want to use a blog program or web developer, it is possible to purchase a website on your own. To do this you will need to purchase a domain name and get your site hosted. The specifics of setting up your own website go beyond the scope of this book. Certain companies like Squarespace (www.squarespace.com) and Intuit (www.intuit.com) now allow you to purchase a domain name, get your site hosted, and set up a basic website. While these do not allow for the most dynamic of sites, it is a good starter guide and relatively inexpensive when compared to hiring your own web developer.

Regardless of which option you choose, you want to make sure that at a minimum your website includes your contact information, location schedule, and menu; all of which is up-to-date so someone doesn't stand on an empty street corner waiting for you when you're actually setting up across town that day!

Do You Need To Pay For Search Engine Optimization?

As soon as you register a domain name and get a website online you will likely start receiving emails from people who swear they can help bring your website to the top of the search rankings for a mere few hundred or thousand dollars. Is it worth it? Well, when was the last time you sifted through three, five, or nine search results pages? Most people look at the search results posted on the first page and that's it.

Prior to 2011, Search Engine Optimization (SEO for short) was one of the hottest things on the internet and, if you hired the right (read, expensive) people, they could normally help raise your ranking to the first page or even the top ranked search result.

However, Google, Bing, and other major search engines changed the algorithm they use for web crawlers in late 2010, which meant that all those tried and true SEO tricks are no longer quite so powerful. This doesn't mean that SEO doesn't have its place, but there are tricks you can use on your own to make your website more easily searchable by web crawlers.

First, as you write the copy for your website, consult Google Adwords (www.google.com/adwords) to find out what some of the most commonly searched words are in your specific niche. For example, if you plan on selling gourmet pies from your food kiosk you may find that the most commonly searched word is apple pie. It would then be beneficial to specifically mention that you offer apple pie, if you in fact do, on the website so that when someone searches for sites relating to apple pie food trucks your site will jump to the top of the list.

One of the newest parts of the web search algorithms is that web crawlers now rank sites that use similar words by how frequently the site is updated and how new the content is. In this case, a blog that's incorporated into your site can be incredibly powerful in helping get your website to the top of search rankings. In addition to providing readers with interesting information

Do You Need To Pay For Search Engine Optimization?

about your company, recent blog posts that use those frequently searched words will improve the rank of your site. In the pie example, if in addition to mentioning you sell apple pies on your website you also write blog posts about how you choose apples for your apple pies, what type of crust goes best with apple pies, and an interview with your apple farmer, then your site will be ranked higher than a website that just mentions their apple pie on a website that hasn't been updated in years. More information about blogging is on page 83.

Before You Log Off

If you're going to spend money and time developing your mobile food company's website, you want to make sure that you can see and understand who is coming to your site and why. Many blog programs have built-in statics that will show you how many people are visiting your site daily, what key phrases are driving people to your site, and where people are visiting from. If the program you use doesn't have this capability or if you're developing a site from scratch, you should be able to integrate it with Google Analytics (www.google.com/analytics) at no cost. Easily one of the most comprehensive web analytical tools available, Google Analytics can provide you with a wealth of information about how people interact with your site that can help guide your online marketing strategy. Given the price, it is well worth the investment!

Blogs

Blog posts not only help tell your story to people, they can also be an effective way to build customer loyalty. In today's world, where people have literally thousands of choices, they are more and more interested in having a connection with a brand or a company rather than simply buying an unknown entity. The way the big mega-brands typically build that connection is through large advertising budgets that broadcast their message and brand image around the country. While blog posts may not reach the same number of people as a large advertising campaign, they are an incredibly powerful way to share your story and your passion with potential customers.

Regardless of whether your blog is incorporated into a separately-hosted website or you use a blog program like WordPress or Blogger for your website already, blog posts work to your benefit in two main ways. First of all, because of changes in search engine algorithms, blog posts that are frequently updated can help potential customers more easily find your site because your website will rank higher in web searches. Secondly, once people either find your site through a web search or are directed to it through other marketing methods, blog posts can keep people engaged in your food company as they learn more about you and your business through the posts.

Though usually free to start, the biggest thing to keep in mind if you plan on using blogs as part of your marketing strategy is there is a considerable amount of time that must be devoted to writing posts to keep your blog fresh. At first, your blog will have few readers. To increase traffic, you must provide valuable content and you must do it on a regular enough schedule that people will want to come back and check your blog frequently and share your content with their friends.

Which leads to the question of what should you include in the blog. It's not uncommon for business owners to question why anyone would find the intricacies of their business interesting. How many times do people want to hear that you're chopping apples for that apple pie? The key to good blog posts is to think broadly about your business. Using the apple pie example again, you could write a post about how to keep your knives sharp for fruit chopping, include an interview with a bee expert who talks about how the bee colony collapse could impact future apple harvests, link to mentions of local amateur apple pie contests, or even include a video that shows you peeling an apple while keeping the peel intact. All of these ideas don't even touch on the easy topics such as how you developed your apple pie recipe or where you get your apples. As you can see, if you look at your business from a broad prospective and ask yourself questions you think readers would want answers to you will come up with a myriad of topics your blog can cover. It is possible to hire a blog copywriter, but the truth of the matter is that no one knows your business as well as you do. If you would like more information about how to fill a blog with powerful content, be sure to check out *Content Rules* by Ann Hadley, C.C. Chapman, and David Meerman Scott.

Facebook

Like all inbound marketing tools, Facebook (www.facebook.com) is about creating one-on-one relationships with people and developing those relationships over time. At this time, Facebook is one the most trafficked websites in the world alongside Google, Bing, and Yahoo. Facebook Pages, which are specific for businesses and different from profiles for individuals, also have the added benefit of being searchable by web search engines so your street cart Facebook Page can help you get found on the internet.

It's important to note that anything you post to your Facebook Page is not actively shared with the entire Facebook world. Someone must become a fan of your page to have your posts show up in their newsfeeds. This means that you must actively work to gain fans. Be sure to include links to your Facebook page on all marketing you do including in email blasts, your website, any advertisements, and even on your mobile unit itself. If you create a Facebook account for your food business, you also can take advantage of Facebook Networks as a way to help you connect with people. Specifically for a mobile food company that does business in a specific city, you can join the networks for that location, which will help people in that area find and fan your Facebook page more easily.

Just like Twitter, which is explained in the next section, the best way to gain a following is by posting interesting and engaging information to your Facebook page. You don't just have to post your newest location or menu, but you can create contests, ask questions, and solicit feedback. If, for example, you're thinking of offering a gluten-free item you can post it on your Facebook page and see if people are excited to try it or not. The businesses that most benefit from Facebook pages are those that actively try to build relationships with fans and listen as much as they talk.

Facebook also can provide you with user analytics that will help you learn more about your fans. You can use this information as you develop future marketing strategies, create new menu items, or even determine new locations to bring your food truck. Not to mention, Facebook also has a very powerful advertising tool that you can use to create pay-per-click ads that can highly target your audience based on specifics you input into the system.

For instance, you may learn through your Facebook user analytics that the majority of your users are college-aged and reside in the university section of town. You could use this information to try and build your fan base and, one hopes your customer base, by creating a Facebook ad that targets college-aged users in that same section of town. Or perhaps 20-something Facebook users throughout the entire city who are alumni of that university. The beauty of Facebook ads is that as you are creating them, Facebook will share with you how many people meet the criteria you're searching for. In this case, Facebook may show that there are 200 college-age users in that section of town, but when you change the age parameter you may see that there are 1,200 people aged 25-30 in that same neighborhood. If you're planning to take your food truck there based on the number of college-aged fans you have on your site, it may make sense to develop a Facebook ad targeting the 25-30 year olds in that area to invite them to come out and try your food when you're in the neighborhood.

Twitter

Some marketers argue that Twitter (www.twitter.com), with its 140-character limit, is nothing more than a platform for people and businesses to scream their message into the void, but done well, Twitter can mobilize your customers and give them a reason to come out to you. Sometimes referred to as micro-blogging, Twitter enables followers to quickly digest what you have to say while making it just as easy for you to update customers on your location, new menu items, or new and interesting news. What makes it different from Facebook is that your "tweets" can literally been seen by everyone on Twitter, whereas Facebook updates are limited to those who are fans of your company.

In addition to "tweeting" your newest or upcoming location, there are several other benefits to using Twitter for your mobile food company. First and foremost, you can build a following. The easiest way to do this, after you have your business set up on Twitter, is to search for people to "follow." Typically, as long as you don't appear to be a spammer, most people on Twitter will follow those who follow them. Start by doing a search for Twitter accounts in your area and see if any of those people might be a good match for your company. If you're based in San Antonio, for example, you might try searching for other

Twitter accounts that are also based in San Antonio and who like gourmet food.

Of course this "following" is a two-way street and you should, in good conscious, follow those who follow you. The exceptions to this are some of the spammers, the "make a million dollars working from home" tweeters, as well as anyone whose tweets become outrageous or offensive.

Speaking of tweets, the way to truly grow a solid Twitter fan base is by sharing information on Twitter that your audience cares about. In addition to your location, which is the most obvious tweet-worthy piece of news for food trucks and food carts, you want to provide your followers with information that benefits them. Everything you post doesn't have to be mobile food-based. Twitter can help you develop a personality and relationship with your followers outside of simply serving them great food. For example, if you read an incredible book about the food industry and think others might like hearing about it, tweet a short review and link to the book. Or if you write a particularly great blog post, then tweet a link to it.

Twitter isn't just about tweeting, though. You want to engage with the people who follow you and learn from those you follow. If you are going to use Twitter as one of the pieces of your marketing strategy then you must be willing to participate in it and not simply post infrequently and never tweet with anyone. That is a sure-fire way to lose your followers' interest.

Another benefit of Twitter is that you can keep track of what people are saying about you, about competitors, and about specific topics. Twitter has a search tool (http://twitter.com/#!/search-home) that you can use to track conversations. Set up searches on your company name, your Twitter handle, phrases specific to your business, and anything else that may be of interest to you. Then when you see someone mention, for example, that they want to know what kind of apples to use in an apple pie, you can tweet-in with a response. Once again, by engaging in the Twitter community in addition to tweeting promotions and your location, you will endear yourself to your Twitter followers. When you realize that each of your followers has tens, hundreds, or even thousands of followers of their own you can quickly see how powerful this tool can be. Your helping one person with their apple choice may be retweeted, which is where someone will repost your tweet to their followers, which will get your company in front of even more people who may decide to follow you, look up your website, or visit your cart for the first time.

Location-Based Marketing

Location-based marketing, through sites like FourSquare (www.foursquare.com) and Gowalla (www.gowalla.com), are a way to incentivize people to visit your food truck, food trailer, or food cart. Currently location-based marketing sites award points to people as they "check in" at various locations. So anytime someone visits your food truck they would check in online and receive a point. The idea was that people would be able to play against one another and their friends and compete to gain the most points over a certain amount of time. I say "was" because some location-based marketing sites are phasing out points because it's become too easy for users to take advantage of the system.

That doesn't mean location-based marketing isn't useful. Customers can leave feedback on your location-based site that may entice new customers to try your food truck. Most of these sites also allow you to post special offers to users and these offers, which are currently free for you to advertise, can be seen by anyone who uses the site. This means that someone looking for great apple pie in his city is able to log in, learn about your street cart, read reviews, and see that you're currently offering a "two slices of pie for $5" promotion. That's a powerful way to catch customers' interest and get them heading in your direction. In fact, this new marketing avenue holds such promise that Groupon and other Daily Deal sites are starting to develop location-based marketing deals for businesses. It also is believed that location-based marketing sites will soon be able to tailor recommendations to users based on their search history and location so that someone who has a history of eating at food trucks and logs in around the corner from where your food truck is currently parked would be alerted to your location.

If you're unsure about how to best to use location-based marketing, do a search for other food trucks and food carts and see how they use it. If you believe this is something your customers use or will use in the future, location-based marketing is worthwhile pursuing. Not sure if your customers use it or not? Try posting a question to your Facebook Page, Twitter account, or via a blog post and see what type of response you get!

Public Relations

Getting your business mentioned in the press can be a wonderful free tool for getting your food company out in front of consumers. If you speak to experienced food entrepreneurs though, you'll often hear that while press may attract attention, it doesn't necessarily always turn into sales. Not to mention that getting written up in the press can't be counted on so don't make press the cornerstone of your marketing strategy.

If you are interested in trying to attract press, there are two main methods you can use. Not unlike outbound and inbound marketing, there also is outbound and inbound PR. Outbound PR includes sending press releases to journalists with information about your product (food samples are always appreciated, too!) in hopes that your company will interest them enough to write a piece about it. There are a few things to keep in mind if you go this route. First, you need to determine who your target journalists or target publications are based on your knowledge of your target audience (do you see a recurring theme here?). For a mobile food business that is looking to serve a local customer base, it wouldn't make sense to send press releases to national publications because they might not have that many readers, listeners, or viewers in your specific region. On the other hand, local outlets like regional magazines, local radio stations, local news or entertainment shows, and area blogs are going to have more of your target audience in it. For example, sending your company information – and perhaps even an invitation to come try your food truck for free – to the writer of a hyper-local neighborhood blog in a section of town that your food truck frequents (who, hopefully, then writes a positive review) is likely to result in significantly more customers visiting your food truck than a mention in *The Washington Post*.

What information should you include in a press release? The short answer is anything that is newsworthy. While a press release should always contain basics like your company information and contact information, the first paragraph needs to contain the who, what, when, where, why, and if applicable, the how of your news piece. In today's increasingly-busy world, journalists simply do not have time to read lengthy press releases. You want to make your headline and first paragraph jump out and grab the reporter, so that they not only want to finish reading your press release but also want to call you for a follow up interview.

Inbound PR, on the other hand, is where you connect directly with reporters who are looking to cover stories that relate to your mobile food company. Thankfully, the Internet and a few enterprising businesspeople have made this process significantly easier than in years past. The leader in reporter-to-source connections is Help A Reporter Out (www.helpareporter.com); also known as HARO for short. This free subscription service attracts journalists from top-notch newspapers, magazines, radio stations, and blogs. These journalists submit their interview and expert requests for stories they are actively working on to HARO, which compiles the requests and emails them out three-times daily to subscribers. All you have to do is look through the requests and determine if any are in line with your business or are on a topic you can speak knowledgeably about and then you contact the journalist directly. While it's important to only answer press requests that fit with your business (i.e. – a journalist who is interested in hedge fund managers really doesn't want to talk to you about your food cart business), and not doing so can get you banned from HARO, you do need to have a creative approach to the definition of your business. Rather than simply limiting yourself to journalists who are looking for food truck owners, your background and experience might also make you a good source for stories about career-changers, people who turned grandma's secret recipe into a business, or small businesses that use social media as a marketing strategy. HARO also has a Twitter account (@helpareporter) where source requests for reporters on tight deadlines will be posted.

Twitter also is a powerful way to keep an eye on the media and make connections when appropriate. If you want to know which reporters and news outlets are on Twitter, check out https://twitteringjournalists.pbwiki.com/Media+Outlets+Using+Twitter and https://twitteringjournalists.pbwiki.com/Media+People+Using +Twitter. You can follow the outlets and people who are relevant to your food business, which will help you learn what types of stories they write about. You also may learn stories journalists are working on ahead of time and can offer yourself up as a source. If there's a journalist in particular that you want to pitch a story idea and they're on Twitter, it is worthwhile to consider pitching them through Twitter. You can send direct messages via Twitter to people you follow if they follow you back. For many of these journalists, the condensed version of Twitter makes it easier for them to quickly read pitches (and forces you to write very tightly worded pitches) and they can immediately decide if they want more information or not.

Interestingly enough, press releases posted on your website also can be a source of inbound PR. Not surprisingly, journalists who are researching specific topics often use the Internet while searching. If your press releases are included in your website and can be read by search engines, your company may pop to the top of a journalist's search. This certainly isn't an everyday occurrence but even if you never send a press release out to any journalist it is useful to write press releases and post them to your site just in case. Not to mention, that if you answer a HARO or Twitter media request the first thing a reporter will likely do is visit your website before contacting you to determine if you are the right fit for their story or not. Having an extensive press release section will show the reporter that your food truck, food cart, or food trailer is a legitimate business and one with a story worth telling.

Final Marketing Thoughts

When it comes to developing a marketing plan you should, like almost every other aspect of building your business, determine who your customers are and what media they do or don't consume. If you find that your customers are very technologically-savvy and spend most of their time on Twitter it would make sense to get a Twitter account and start building relationships there. However, if your audience prefers more traditional media you might be better off developing a marketing plan that is heavy on traditional outbound marketing.

The best thing about being a small food business, though, is that what you may lack in ad dollars you make up for by being nimble. You can try out different marketing techniques to see if they work for you and if they don't, you can quickly change strategy. A little trial-and-error can help you find the right mix. Try to stay abreast of ever-evolving marketing tools as much as possible so that, when its right for your customers, your mobile food business is at the forefront of new marketing technology.

Whatever methods or combination of methods you use to share your marketing message, be sure that your plans are fully integrated. This means that if you plan on using, for example, Facebook, make sure that there's a link from your company website to your Facebook page. If you send out an e-newsletter and have a Twitter account, you can share the newsletter on Twitter. Not to mention that the e-newsletter should include a link to your Twitter account. Making sure that whatever marketing tools you use connect to each other will give people more opportunities to not only find you, but to contact and stay connected with you in the method they prefer.

The Business Financials

When you were first learning to drive you likely had to read a little booklet that explained everything you needed to know about how to be a safe driver before taking a test. Starting a food truck business is no different only that the test you're trying to pass is getting the business going and making it profitable. Just as understanding it's important to stop at red lights, understanding the financials of your business is key to making your company successful.

Product Cost Analysis

First and foremost you have to understand how much it costs you to make your products. Product pricing is a key component to building a successful business, but it's one that too many people simply skim over. It's not unusual for food entrepreneurs to not know how much their product truly costs and simply charge what they anticipate to be a fair price for an item. However, if you don't know how much it costs to make the product then you can't know if the price you charge will actually make you any money.

To determine your product costs follow the steps below for each of your menu items. A sample product spreadsheet is on page 97 for reference and a product cost worksheet to use with your products is available in Appendix V on page 150. The following information is based on the fictional company Sweet Bits Treat Truck outlined in the Sample Business Plan in Appendix 1 on page 133.

Step 1A: Ingredient Unit Cost: Divide the total cost you paid for each ingredient (including tax if applicable) by the total number of units bought. For example, if a 5-pound bag of flour costs $4.80 then the unit cost is $.06 per ounce:

5 LB x 16 = 80 ounces (there are 16 ounces in a pound so this converts the units to ounces)

$4.80 (total unit cost)/80 ounces = $0.06 per ounce

Step 1B: Product Ingredient Cost: To determine the unit cost of each ingredient in each product, multiply the number of units you use in a recipe with the corresponding ingredients Unit Cost from Step 1A. Using the above example, if you use 5 ounces of flour in your recipe then the Product Ingredient Cost is $0.30.

5 (ounces of flour) x $.06 (Ingredient Unit Cost) = $0.30

Step 1C: Total Ingredient Cost: Add together all the Product Ingredient Costs to arrive at the Total Ingredient Cost

Step 1D: Per Piece Total Ingredient Cost: Divide the Total Ingredient Costs by the number of units each recipe makes to get your Per Piece Total Ingredient Cost. If your Total Ingredient Cost comes to $2.19 and the recipe makes 12 pieces, then your Per Piece Total Ingredient Cost is $0.18 per piece.

$2.19 (Total Ingredient Cost)/12(Total Units) = $0.18

Your product likely also has some type of packaging cost associated with it. Whether that is a takeout container, wax paper or just a popsicle stick, you likely will have some packaging costs that should be added into your Per Piece Total Ingredient Cost.

Step 2: Packaging Cost: Add together any packaging costs for the product including bags, takeout containers, etc. on a per-unit basis to arrive at your total packaging cost per product. If you will be packaging your items in a takeout box that costs $0.29 and will include a label on the box that costs $0.06 then your total packaging cost is $0.35 per unit

$.29 (takeout box) + $0.06 (label) = $0.35

Step 3: Total Product Cost: To arrive at your Total Product Cost, multiply the number of products per package by the Total Ingredient Cost and add in the Total Packaging Cost. For example, if you will be selling three cookies which cost you $0.18 per cookies, then your Total Product Cost including your packaging will be $0.89.

$0.18 (cookies Ingredient Cost) x 3 = $0.54

$0.54 + $0.35 (Total Packaging Cost) = $0.89

Sweet Bits Treat Truck
Product Cost

Chocolate Inferno Cookies
Product Cost

Ingredients	Amount Used (ounces)	Per Unit Cost	Total
gluten-free flour	5	$ 0.30	$ 1.50
cocoa powder	0.33	$ 0.13	$ 0.04
butter	8	$ 0.04	$ 0.32
eggs (per egg)	2	$ 0.15	$ 0.30
cayenne pepper	0.12	$ 0.29	$ 0.03
Total Ingredient Cost			$ 2.19
Per Piece Product Ingredient Cost (12 pieces)			$ 0.18

Packaging

Packaging	Amount Used	Per Unit Cost	Total
Labels	1	$ 0.06	$ 0.06
Takeout Box	1	$ 0.29	$ 0.29
Total Product Packaging Cost			$ 0.35

Number of Cookies per package			3
Total Per Package Ingredient Cost			$ 0.54
Total Product Cost with Packaging			$ 0.89

Pricing Your Menu

Once you know exactly how much it costs you to produce your products you know what price, at a minimum, you need to sell them to break even. However, this price does not take into account all the costs associated with running your business such as the cost of your or an employee's time to make the product or the price of gas in the case of a food truck. To get to a starting place for pricing, the industry rule of thumb is that you should quadruple your Total Product Cost to arrive at a ballpark retail price. If you plan on also selling your food via wholesale channels then try doubling your Total Product Cost to arrive at a starting wholesale price.

As noted above, this is really only a starting price because there are other factors that aren't directly related to your Total Product Costs, such as how many staff members it takes to prep, prepare, and serve the item, what prices for similar items are like in your area, and how much you think customers will be willing to pay. It will be an uphill battle to get customers to pay $20 for your gourmet burgers if every other restaurant and food truck selling burgers charges $10 or less.

Determining proper prices for the items on your menu can take a little bit of trial and error and you shouldn't hesitate to raise or lower prices slightly if you can. At the end of the day, the best way to make money is to serve the greatest number of people at a price point that maximizes your profit margin. You may find that a lower price point brings more people to your food truck but you need to make sure that you're making money with each item you sell, which is why understanding your Total Product Costs are so critical.

Sweet Bits Treat Truck
Product Cost and Pricing

Chocolate Inferno Cookies
Product Cost

Ingredients	Amount Used (ounces)	Per Unit Cost	Total
gluten-free flour	5	$ 0.30	$ 1.50
cocoa powder	0.33	$ 0.13	$ 0.04
butter	8	$ 0.04	$ 0.32
eggs (per egg)	2	$ 0.15	$ 0.30
cayenne pepper	0.12	$ 0.29	$ 0.03
Total Ingredient Cost			$ 2.19
Per Piece Product Ingredient Cost (12 pieces)			$ 0.18

Packaging

Packaging	Amount Used	Per Unit Cost	Total
Labels	1	$ 0.06	$ 0.06
Takeout Box	1	$ 0.29	$ 0.29
Total Product Packaging Cost			$ 0.35

Number of Cookies per package	3
Total Per Package Ingredient Cost	$ 0.54
Total Product Cost with Packaging	$ 0.89

Product Pricing

Sales Channel	Cost	Price Charged	Profit
Individual Cookie	$ 0.18	$ 2.00	$ 1.82
Packaged Cookies	$ 0.89	$ 5.00	$ 4.11

Cash Forecasting

Knowing how much to charge for your products is one thing but before starting up your business you should have a good idea of how much you'll be spending on a monthly basis and how much you anticipate earning. Business plan books tell you that when starting a business, you need to build out an income statement and balance sheet. While helpful, for an independently-owned food truck business the focus should really be on cash forecasting. How much money or liquidity the business has at any given time is incredibly important to a small business as a healthy cash position will enable you to pay your bills on time and keep the day-to-day business running. Even if you anticipate great sales in the future, without cash in the bank you won't be able to fill up your truck's tank with gas and get out in front of your customers today. Developing a cash forecast will show you how and when money will be spent along with how and when you anticipate receiving cash from sales. Then you can make sure that the two add up so that your business always has cash available when needed.

When creating a cash forecast, the first thing you need to know is what your monthly operating costs will most likely be. Operating costs differ from your startup costs in that they typically occur on a monthly basis or otherwise regular basis whereas startup costs are one-time, initial upfront costs to get the business up and running. For example, if you lease your food truck then you will likely have a monthly lease payment that's due. If you purchase your food truck, that cost would be seen as a startup cost because you will only make that large lump payment once. However, if you take out a loan to purchase your food truck you will have monthly payments that will be due to the bank that should be considered part of your monthly operating costs.

There are two types of operating costs – fixed operating costs and variable operating costs. Fixed operating costs are things that will occur every month regardless of if you have any sales. These are things like your phone bill, your monthly web hosting fees, your truck lease payment or bank loan payment, and any rent owed for your commissary or kitchen space. Variable operating costs depend on how much business you're doing — the cost of your ingredients, gas for the truck and any discretionary expenses that you can easily increase or decrease such as how much you spend on advertising. It's important to remember the difference between the two because if your sales go up your fixed operating costs are going to remain unchanged, but your variable operating costs that correspond with your product, mainly ingredient and packaging costs and possibly gas costs if you are moving the truck frequently, will increase. On the same note, if you aren't making a lot of food then your variable operating costs will be minimal but your fixed operating costs will stay the same regardless.

The following page provides an example of the fixed and variable costs for the fictional company Sweet Bits Treat Truck. From this you can see how Sweet Bits anticipates what the average monthly cash needs will be over and above startup costs for the first six months in business.

Sweet Bits Treat Truck
Realistic Cash Forecast

	Startup	May	June	July	Aug	Sept	Oct
Fixed Costs							
Food Truck w/ Equipment	$ 75,000	$ -	$ -	$ -	$ -	$ -	$ -
Kitchen Facilities / Commissary	$ -	$ 750	$ 750	$ 750	$ 750	$ 750	$ 750
Office Supplies	$ 150	$ 150	$ 150	$ 150	$ 150	$ 150	$ 150
Telephone/Internet	$ 110	$ 110	$ 110	$ 110	$ 110	$ 110	$ 110
Loan Repayment	$ 893	$ 893	$ 893	$ 893	$ 893	$ 893	$ 893
Accounting	$ -	$ 40	$ 40	$ 40	$ 40	$ 40	$ 40
Total Monthly Fixed Costs	$ 76,153	$ 1,943	$ 1,943	$ 1,943	$ 1,943	$ 1,943	$ 1,943
Variable Costs							
Ingredients	$ -	$ 1,250	$ 1,500	$ 1,750	$ 1,750	$ 1,500	$ 1,250
Gas	$ -	$ 347	$ 441	$ 510	$ 510	$ 441	$ 347
Parking Fees	$ -	$ 125	$ 230	$ 315	$ 315	$ 230	$ 125
Marketing							
Farmers' Market Minimum Fee	$ -	$ 180	$ 210	$ 240	$ 240	$ 210	$ 180
Print Advertising	$ -	$ -	$ -	$ -	$ -	$ -	$ -
Online Advertising	$ -	$ 25	$ 25	$ 25	$ 25	$ 25	$ 25
Newsletter/e-newsletter	$ -	$ -	$ -	$ -	$30	$ -	$ -
Marketing Postcards	$ 600	$ -	$ -	$ -	$ -	$ -	$ -
Website	$ 3,000	$ -	$ -	$ -	$ -	$ -	$ -
Photography	$ 800	$ -	$ -	$ -	$ -	$ -	$ -
Truck Wrap	$ 2,500	$ -	$ -	$ -	$ -	$ -	$ -
Total Variable Costs	$ 6,900	$ 1,927	$ 2,406	$ 2,840	$ 2,870	$ 2,406	$ 1,927
Payroll							
Paychecks	$ -	$ 3,120	$ 3,900	$ 4,680	$ 4,680	$ 3,900	$ 3,120
Payroll Costs	$ 200	$ 52	$ 52	$ 52	$ 52	$ 52	$ 52
Payroll Taxes	$ -	$ 468	$ 585	$ 702	$ 702	$ 585	$ 468
Payroll Total	$ 200	$ 3,640	$ 4,537	$ 5,434	$ 5,434	$ 4,537	$ 3,640
Other Costs							
Packaging Costs							
Labels	$ 350	$ -	$ -	$ -	$ -	$ -	$ -
Compostable Bags	$ 200	$ -	$ -	$ -	$ -	$ -	$ -
Compostable Forks	$ 150	$ -	$ -	$ -	$ -	$ -	$ -
Business Licenses	$ 500	$ -	$ -	$ -	$ -	$ -	$ -
Health Permits	$ 650	$ -	$ -	$ -	$ -	$ -	$ -
Total Other Costs	$ 1,850	$ -	$ -	$ -	$ -	$ -	$ -
Total Operating Costs	$ 85,103	$ 7,510	$ 8,886	$ 10,217	$ 10,247	$ 8,886	$ 7,510

As you can see in the above example, Sweet Bits Treat Truck anticipates that the fixed operating costs will remain the same every month during the summer but her variable costs, mainly the ingredients and gas budget, will rise during the peak of summer and decrease in the spring and fall when the weather is less reliable and people may be less willing to head outdoors for their treats.

It's also important to note that Sweet Bits has taken into account the fact that there are several costs that will have to be paid in May for things like packaging, truck wrapping, and marketing material. Even though these items may be used all year long, it will be necessary for Sweet Bits to have an adequate amount of cash on hand or a business credit card to pay for those items before business is anticipated to pick up in the summer.

Once you understand your monthly expenses, you need to add in what you think you will sell on a monthly basis to get a true cash forecast. Without any historical data behind you, this really is your best guess as to how much you may sell during any given month taking into account how much of the product you can physically make and how densely populated the locations are you plan on visiting. There's no use putting into your projection that you'll serve 20,000 customers a month if it is physically impossible for you to produce that much. If you have multiple price points on your menu for different items you should get the average price of all items and use that as your per-unit price. While it won't be entirely accurate as some people will spend more and some will spend less, this will give you a ballpark figure you can use in your projections. In future years, once you have a sales history, you can revise this based on the true average customer bill. One recommendation is to make three projections based on 1) a worst-case sales scenario, 2) a "real" scenario based on what you actually anticipate selling and 3) a best-case sales scenario. Keep in mind as your sales change in each of those scenarios so too will some of your variable costs. Note the change in the cost of ingredients, gas, and employee time in each of the following three sample projections.

Sweet Bits Treat Truck
Realistic Cash Forecast

	Startup	May	June	July	Aug	Sept
Fixed Costs						
Food Truck w/ Equipment	$ 60,000	$ -	$ -	$ -	$ -	$ -
Kitchen Facilities / Commissary	$ -	$ 750	$ 750	$ 750	$ 750	$ 750
Office Supplies	$ 150	$ 150	$ 150	$ 150	$ 150	$ 150
Telephone/Internet	$ 110	$ 110	$ 110	$ 110	$ 110	$ 110
Loan Repayment	$ 893	$ 893	$ 893	$ 893	$ 893	$ 893
Accounting	$ -	$ 40	$ 40	$ 40	$ 40	$ 40
Total Monthly Fixed Costs	$ 61,153	$ 1,943	$ 1,943	$ 1,943	$ 1,943	$ 1,943
Variable Costs						
Ingredients	$ -	$ 1,250	$ 1,500	$ 1,750	$ 1,750	$ 1,500
Gas	$ -	$ 347	$ 441	$ 510	$ 510	$ 441
Parking Fees	$ -	$ 125	$ 230	$ 315	$ 315	$ 230
Marketing						
Farmers' Market Minimum Fee	$ -	$ 180	$ 210	$ 240	$ 240	$ 210
Print Advertising	$ -	$ -	$ -	$ -	$ -	$ -
Online Advertising	$ -	$ 25	$ 25	$ 25	$ 25	$ 25
Newsletter/e-newsletter	$ -	$ -	$ -	$ -	$30	$ -
Marketing Postcards	$ 600	$ -	$ -	$ -	$ -	$ -
Website	$ 3,000	$ -	$ -	$ -	$ -	$ -
Photography	$ 800	$ -	$ -	$ -	$ -	$ -
Truck Wrap	$ 2,500	$ -	$ -	$ -	$ -	$ -
Total Variable Costs	$ 6,900	$ 1,927	$ 2,406	$ 2,840	$ 2,870	$ 2,406
Payroll						
Paychecks	$ -	$ 3,120	$ 3,900	$ 4,680	$ 4,680	$ 3,900
Payroll Costs	$ 200	$ 52	$ 52	$ 52	$ 52	$ 52
Payroll Taxes	$ -	$ 468	$ 585	$ 702	$ 702	$ 585
Payroll Total	$ 200	$ 3,640	$ 4,537	$ 5,434	$ 5,434	$ 4,537
Other Costs						
Packaging Costs						
Labels	$ 350	$ -	$ -	$ -	$ -	$ -
Compostable Bags	$ 200	$ -	$ -	$ -	$ -	$ -
Compostable Forks	$ 150	$ -	$ -	$ -	$ -	$ -
Business Licenses	$ 500	$ -	$ -	$ -	$ -	$ -
Health Permits	$ 650	$ -	$ -	$ -	$ -	$ -
Total Other Costs	$ 1,850	$ -	$ -	$ -	$ -	$ -
Total Operating Costs	$ 70,103	$ 7,510	$ 8,886	$ 10,217	$ 10,247	$ 8,886
Projected Sales	$ -	$ 11,250	$ 13,500	$ 15,750	$ 15,750	$ 13,500
Net Income (Sales - Costs)	$ (70,103)	$ 3,740	$ 4,614	$ 5,533	$ 5,503	$ 4,614
Starting Cash On Hand	$ 100,000	$ 29,897	$ 33,637	$ 38,251	$ 43,784	$ 49,287
+ Net Income	$ 29,897	$ 33,637	$ 38,251	$ 43,784	$ 49,287	$ 53,901
Ending Cash On Hand	$ 29,897	$ 33,637	$ 38,251	$ 43,784	$ 49,287	$ 53,901

In the above "realistic" case, Sweet Bits Treat Truck starts with $100,000 in available cash. However, this money must cover all the startup costs as well as fund operating costs once the business gets going. Even though after five months, the business has less cash on hand when it started, it's important to note that this is mainly due to the one-time startup costs. In fact, the business owner anticipates making a profit every month over and above the monthly loan payments and all employee expenses. Not included in these employee expenses though, is any payment to the entrepreneur directly. In this scenario, the owner would be able to take a monthly draw from the business to pay him/herself or might choose instead to put additional money towards the loan to pay it down faster. Also notice that as summer gets into full swing, it's anticipated that sales will increase as more people hear about the business. The business owner should continue the monthly cash forecast for a full 12 months to estimate how much sales might decrease in the winter and how much cash should be available to cover fixed costs during those potentially slower months.

	Startup	May	June	July	Aug	Sept
Fixed Costs						
Food Truck w/ Equipment	$ 60,000	$ -	$ -	$ -	$ -	$ -
Kitchen Facilities / Commissary	$ -	$ 750	$ 750	$ 750	$ 750	$ 750
Office Supplies	$ 150	$ 150	$ 150	$ 150	$ 150	$ 150
Telephone/Internet	$ 110	$ 110	$ 110	$ 110	$ 110	$ 110
Loan Repayment	$ 893	$ 893	$ 893	$ 893	$ 893	$ 893
Accounting	$ -	$ 40	$ 40	$ 40	$ 40	$ 40
Total Monthly Fixed Costs	**$ 61,153**	**$ 1,943**	**$ 1,943**	**$ 1,943**	**$ 1,943**	**$ 1,943**
Variable Costs						
Ingredients	$ -	$ 940	$ 1,128	$ 1,316	$ 1,316	$ 1,128
Gas	$ -	$ 347	$ 405	$ 515	$ 515	$ 405
Parking Fees	$ -	$ 166	$ 222	$ 312	$ 312	$ 222
Marketing						
Farmers' Market Minimum Fee	$ -	$ 120	$ 140	$ 160	$ 160	$ 140
Print Advertising	$ -	$ -	$ -	$ -	$ -	$ -
Online Advertising	$ -	$ 25	$ 25	$ 25	$ 20	$ 20
Newsletter/e-newsletter	$ -	$ -	$ -	$ -	$30	$ -
Marketing Postcards	$ 600	$ -	$ -	$ -	$ -	$ -
Website	$ 3,000	$ -	$ -	$ -	$ -	$ -
Photography	$ 800	$ -	$ -	$ -	$ -	$ -
Truck Wrap	$ 2,500	$ -	$ -	$ -	$ -	$ -
Total Variable Costs	**$ 6,900**	**$ 1,598**	**$ 1,920**	**$ 2,328**	**$ 2,353**	**$ 1,915**
Payroll						
Paychecks	$ -	$ 1,560	$ 1,950	$ 2,340	$ 2,340	$ 1,950
Payroll Costs	$ 200	$ 52	$ 52	$ 52	$ 52	$ 52
Payroll Taxes	$ -	$ 234	$ 293	$ 351	$ 351	$ 293
Payroll Total	**$ 200**	**$ 1,846**	**$ 2,295**	**$ 2,743**	**$ 2,743**	**$ 2,295**
Other Costs						
Packaging Costs						
Labels	$ 450	$ -	$ -	$ -	$ -	$ -
Compostable Bags	$ 500	$ -	$ -	$ -	$ -	$ -
Compostable Forks	$ 500	$ -	$ -	$ -	$ -	$ -
Business Licenses	$ 500	$ -	$ -	$ -	$ -	$ -
Health Permits	$ 650	$ -	$ -	$ -	$ -	$ -
Total Other Costs	**$ 2,600**	**$ -**	**$ -**	**$ -**	**$ -**	**-**
Total Operating Costs	**$ 70,853**	**$ 5,387**	**$ 6,157**	**$ 7,014**	**$ 7,039**	**$ 6,152**
Projected Sales	**$ -**	**$ 3,759**	**$ 4,511**	**$ 6,579**	**$ 7,895**	**$ 7,895**
Net Income (Sales - Costs)	**$ (70,853)**	**$ (1,628)**	**$ (1,646)**	**$ (435)**	**$ 856**	**$ 1,742**
Starting Cash On Hand	**$ 100,000**	**$ 29,147**	**$ 27,519**	**$ 25,873**	**$ 25,438**	**$ 26,294**
+ Net Income	**$ 29,147**	**$ 27,519**	**$ 25,873**	**$ 25,438**	**$ 26,294**	**$ 28,037**
Ending Cash On Hand	**$ 29,147**	**$ 27,519**	**$ 25,873**	**$ 25,438**	**$ 26,294**	**$ 28,037**

The Worst-case Cash Forecast shows what would happen if customers are slow to get excited about Sweet Bits' treats. As you can see, it's not a pretty sight and before moving forward the entrepreneur

— and you, if your worst-case looks like this — needs to ask if s/he can handle losing most of the initial investment into the business should the worst-case scenario prove true. However, you may notice that starting in August the entrepreneur anticipates making a profit each month. As such, the entrepreneur may believe that sales will continue to grow month over month.

It should be noted that if at any point in making any of your projections you show a negative amount in either the starting or ending cash on hand that means the business will not have enough money to pay its obligations and additional cash will need to be injected into the business. You want to be sure that your business either has enough cash or that you are able to supply enough cash to tide you over during those low periods. Keep in mind that one of the major reasons small businesses fail is that they underestimate the level of capital or cash needed to startup and maintain the business.

Sweet Bits Treat Truck
Best Case Cash Forecast

	Startup	May	June	July	Aug	Sept
Fixed Costs						
Food Truck w/ Equipment	$ 60,000	$ -	$ -	$ -	$ -	$ -
Kitchen Facilities / Commissary	$ -	$ 750	$ 750	$ 750	$ 750	$ 750
Office Supplies	$ 150	$ 150	$ 150	$ 150	$ 150	$ 150
Telephone/Internet	$ 110	$ 110	$ 110	$ 110	$ 110	$ 110
Loan Repayment	$ 893	$ 893	$ 893	$ 893	$ 893	$ 893
Accounting	$ -	$ 40	$ 40	$ 40	$ 40	$ 40
Total Monthly Fixed Costs	$ 61,153	$ 1,943	$ 1,943	$ 1,943	$ 1,943	$ 1,943
Variable Costs						
Ingredients	$ -	$ 1,880	$ 2,256	$ 2,632	$ 2,632	$ 2,256
Gas	$ -	$ 462	$ 587	$ 678	$ 678	$ 587
Parking Fees	$ -	$ 166	$ 306	$ 419	$ 419	$ 306
Marketing						
Farmers' Market Minimum Fee	$ -	$ 240	$ 280	$ 320	$ 320	$ 280
Print Advertising	$ -	$ -	$ -	$ -	$ -	$ -
Online Advertising	$ -	$ 40	$ 40	$ 40	$ 40	$ 40
Newsletter/e-newsletter	$ -	$ -	$ -	$ -	$60	$ -
Marketing Postcards	$ 600	$ -	$ -	$ -	$ -	$ -
Website	$ 3,000	$ -	$ -	$ -	$ -	$ -
Photography	$ 800	$ -	$ -	$ -	$ -	$ -
Truck Wrap	$ 2,500	$ -	$ -	$ -	$ -	$ -
Total Variable Costs	$ 6,900	$ 2,787	$ 3,468	$ 4,089	$ 4,149	$ 3,468
Payroll						
Paychecks	$ -	$ 4,150	$ 5,187	$ 6,224	$ 6,224	$ 5,187
Payroll Costs	$ 200	$ 52	$ 52	$ 52	$ 52	$ 52
Payroll Taxes	$ -	$ 622	$ 778	$ 934	$ 934	$ 778
Payroll Total	$ 200	$ 4,824	$ 6,017	$ 7,210	$ 7,210	$ 6,017
Other Costs						
Packaging Costs						
Labels	$ 450	$ -	$ -	$ -	$ -	$ -
Compostable Bags	$ 500	$ -	$ -	$ -	$ -	$ -
Compostable Forks	$ 500	$ -	$ -	$ -	$ -	$ -
Business Licenses	$ 500	$ -	$ -	$ -	$ -	$ -
Health Permits	$ 650	$ -	$ -	$ -	$ -	$ -
Total Other Costs	$ 2,600	$ -	$ -	$ -	$ -	$ -
Total Operating Costs	$ 70,853	$ 9,554	$ 11,428	$ 13,242	$ 13,302	$ 11,428
Projected Sales	$ -	$ 19,737	$ 23,684	$ 27,632	$ 27,632	$ 23,684
Net Income (Sales - Costs)	$ (70,853)	$ 10,182	$ 12,256	$ 14,390	$ 14,330	$ 12,256
Starting Cash On Hand	$ 100,000	$ 29,147	$ 39,329	$ 51,585	$ 65,975	$ 80,305
+ Net Income	$ 29,147	$ 39,329	$ 51,585	$ 65,975	$ 80,305	$ 92,561
Ending Cash On Hand	$ 29,147	$ 39,329	$ 51,585	$ 65,975	$ 80,305	$ 92,561

However, if things go really well as evidenced by this Best-Case Cash Forecast, Sweet Bits Treat Truck would be able to almost fully re-coop the startup costs in five months. In fact, if this cash forecast is extended to include the rest of the year, it is possible that by the end of Year 1 this business will be profitable. Given that Sweet Bits anticipates selling more food in this scenario, note how the Variable Costs change in this case given that the business would have to buy more ingredients and would owe more to the farmers' market association every week. Once again, the business owner would be able to use the monthly profit to pay him/herself or start paying down the loan earlier and decrease the food truck's monthly fixed costs.

When it comes to cash forecasting there are certainly no guarantees, but by creating a realistic, best-case, and worst-case scenario, you'll be able to better determine if you can financially and emotionally handle the ups and downs of cash flow whether business is better, worse or just as you planned.

Income Statements

Another financial statement used by business owners is a projected income statement (also referred to as a profit and loss statement) provides you with a reality check to help determine if your business is financially sound and will be something investors and bankers will want to see if you look for funding from an outside party. Obviously, when starting up a new business, many of the figures you'll input into a projected Income Statement are estimates based on research you've done and, when in doubt, your best guess. However, the income statement should correspond with the cash forecast in that anticipated expenses and revenue hopefully shouldn't differ materially between the two.

Don't be alarmed if in the first year net income isn't as much as you anticipated or is even negative. The first year for any business is a year of building and learning and you incur most of the startup expenses at that time. While for a mobile food business the startup costs are considerably less than traditional food businesses, there are certain things, such as the mobile unit itself, marketing materials, and a website that you need to spend money on in Year 1 but that can be used in Year 2 and beyond. If at all possible, create projected income statements for the next several years to determine when exactly your business will break even and when it will become profitable and make sure you are comfortable with that number.

Balance Sheets

Often referred to as a snapshot of a company's financial position, the balance sheet provides you with a picture of your business' assets, liabilities, and net worth at a specific point in time, for example, at month or year end. A business' net worth, or owner's equity, is calculated by taking into account all assets that have monetary value whether it be cash, inventory, accounts receivable (money that is owed to the business from customers and clients), and any equipment or real property the business may own and subtracting all liabilities and debts the business has. The difference between the total assets and the total liabilities is the equity or net worth of the company.

Since a balance sheet highlights a company's financial health at a specific date, a projected balance sheet for a startup business is less critical because you will have to fill it with figures based on assumptions that may very well change before the designated date occurs. While useful to a certain degree, the real benefit of a projected balance sheet is being able to use it when seeking outside funding for your business. After starting your business, balance sheets are very useful when used in combination with your income statement to gauge your company's financial performance. A projected Balance Sheet Worksheet is on page 157.

Accounting

All these numbers may have your mind spinning. You want to start a mobile food business because you love food but the truth is you need to understand the financials and be able to keep track of every penny if you want to actually make money at this. Knowing how and why your money is spent and earned is important in helping you make strategic decisions like how much money to allocate to advertising or whether you need to spend more time in Location B as opposed to Location A, because the former is more profitable.

As soon as you are ready to open shop you should create a separate bank account for the business. This will help keep your personal and your business finances separate and make it easier to keep your business records straight. Once you have a business bank account in place you should devise a recordkeeping system that will allow you to track all your expenses and all of your sales. If you already have a strong grasp of your personal finances and keep track of every penny, this shouldn't be too hard for you. However, if you use the "check what the ATM says my balance is before spending any money" method of record keeping you may need to spend a little more time on devising a system that will work for you.

One of the easiest ways, and how many small businesses keep track of their finances, is to invest in an accounting software program designed specifically for small businesses. QuickBooks (www.quickbooks.intuit.com) and Quicken (www.quicken.intuit.com) are two of the most popular software packages currently on the market. This software helps you keep track of all of your expenses and revenue. As long as you keep it up to date, you always have an immediate snapshot of how your business is performing. These systems also can take the information you input and create income statements and balance sheets for you.

If however bookkeeping isn't your strong suit, you may find it worth your peace of mind to hire someone else to keep your accounting books up to date. While it is an added expense, a bookkeeper will help keep your finances organized and make sure that all sales and receipts are entered in a timely manner so you always have the most up-to-date financial information about your business available. A bookkeeper also can help prepare your business' tax documents or refer you to an accountant who can do that work for you if your tax preparation is more complex.

Regardless of whether you hire an accountant or not, you should at the very least consult one. Depending on how you've structured and registered your business there are a multitude of small tax regulations that should be taken under consideration when filing your business taxes. For example, did you know that any money you invest into your business to get it started can usually be written into the business as a loan? This means that when the business is able to repay the loan you won't be taxed on the principal loan amount repaid. As a sole proprietor, partnership, or LLC, you also can usually write off any business losses on your personal income taxes. There are numerous small, but crucial rules that an accountant can help you sort through to make sure that any state and federal business taxes are filed correctly and that you are taking full advantage of the available business deductions.

A Final Note On Financials

If you're not numbers-driven, the concept of cash forecasts, income statements, and balance sheets may seem overwhelming. However, these tools are critical in helping you decide whether your business is viable before you start and crucial in helping you keep it on strong footing once the business is up and running. And with the help of business accounting software like Quicken or QuickBooks, or a skilled bookkeeper, you will be able to keep track of any money spent or earned by the business. Because it's so important, you should plan to review your company's financials on a regular basis, be it daily, weekly, or monthly and compare those results to the prior weeks, months, and years. This will help you quickly identify how your business is growing and allow you to take any remedial steps as needed. Think of this as taking the financial pulse of your business on a regular basis.

Hiring Employees

Between doing all the menu planning, cooking, driving, selling, serving, accounting, and marketing, you may find yourself a little short on time. Running the business, operating the business, and still having time for some type of life may mean that you need to hire one or more employees to help you. There are likely two types of employees you would end up looking for – either kitchen help to assist in any off-site or on-location food preparation and/or frontline employees who will be responsible for taking orders, expediting (telling the cooks what orders they need to prepare), making change and doing it all with an eye towards exceptional customer service. Sometimes you may even be lucky enough to find people who can do both roles well.

To decide how many employees you need to hire, take an inventory of everything that needs to be done from menu planning and buying the ingredients to getting the product served to customers and calculate how many employees you may need on any given day. Be sure to take into consideration the fact that you may need more help on certain days — such as the weekends or other times when you anticipate increased customer traffic — and may be able to work by yourself on other days or during slower times of the year. Keep in mind that you don't necessarily have to pull your food truck out of the garage seven days a week or even every month of the year. You may live in an area of the country where Sundays are a day of religious services and family dinners, in which case your food truck may get little to no business. Or you may be planning to sell gourmet ice cream in Minneapolis which, in the winter, would literally be like trying to sell ice cream to an Eskimo, so your time may be better spent working on something else (or driving your food truck south to a warmer winter location and setting up shop there!). While it's nice to think that you'll be able to work on the business every single day – and you will be there 24/7 in the early days of the business – once things settle into a routine you'd like to at least allocate one day off a week to give yourself a break and to make sure you don't burn out.

Once you know how many employees you need, you should write up a description for each job and start hunting around for help. You can start by posting the job descriptions on Craigslist (www.craigslist.com) and by asking at local culinary programs and colleges. High-school students may also be interested in working for you during the summer months to make a little extra cash.

When you interview potential employees you should look for people who have the skills the job requires and who will embody and represent your brand and your company as you would like. These will be the people who are out in front of the public "selling" your product! It's oftentimes incredibly hard for food truck and food cart entrepreneurs to fully hand off the reigns to new employees because your business literally depends on how well these employees interact with customers. It behooves you to take the time to find people you trust.

Before you hire any employees make sure that you fully understand the hiring requirements set by the government. The IRS website (www.irs.gov) lays out the information you will need to collect from new employees as well as copies of the forms that any new employees must fill out before beginning work.

The truth of the matter is that the hardest part of being an employer isn't hiring people but actually keeping them on staff. If you've spent any time working in professional kitchens then you know that the food industry has an incredibly high turnover of employees. Chances are that most people you hire to work for you don't have any long-term plans about working on your food truck. By using good management techniques and developing an incentive plan though, you may be able to minimize employee turnover.

For example, if your business is busiest during the summer and you have little time to train new employees, you may offer current employees a bonus in addition to their paycheck if they work through Labor Day without quitting. Alternatively, you may find that one employee desperately wants to have solid management experience to put on his resume, so give him a chance to grow by providing him with management opportunities within your company. The best ways to hold onto your staff when you need it most is to listen to your employees, figure out what it is they want from the job, and try to provide it.

Hiring Employees

Remember, when you first register your business with your state you will likely be asked if you plan to hire employees. If you know from the get-go you will hire employees you should check that box. Don't worry if you decide at a later date to hire help because you can always file that change with the state government. Just know that once you alert the government to the possibility that you may hire employees, you will be required to complete monthly and/or quarterly employer reports and file them with the state even if you have no employees at that time.

Payroll & Tax Implications

If you hire employees then you obviously have to pay them. In fact, along those same lines, you have to decide if you want a regular paycheck as well. If you have registered your mobile food business as an S Corp you may be required by law to give yourself a paycheck, but if you are an LLC or sole proprietor you may decide that it makes more sense to take a draw (i.e., a payment) from the business when there is excess cash in the bank and not take money when there are numerous bills that have to be paid or cash is low. If you plan on paying anyone, yourself and/or employees, you will need to set up some type of payroll system.

Unfortunately, taxes have gotten so complex that's it no longer really possible to simply write someone a check for their hours worked. Tax forms filed by employees when they begin working for you will indicate how much of their paycheck should be withheld for income taxes. You will also need to withhold Medicare and Social Security (FICA) payments, both of which are dependent on how much money that employee is making. QuickBooks and Quicken both have employee payroll functions built into the more advanced levels of the software systems. It's also possible to contract with a small payroll company who will prepare your company's paychecks with the appropriate withholding amounts taken into account.

In addition to the paychecks, any payroll service or company you use should also have the capability to produce any monthly or quarterly employer statements you need. As an employer, you not only must turn in your employees' paycheck withholdings to the government, you also are responsible for employer taxes such as unemployment and workers compensation. These monthly or quarterly reports should outline for you how much your mobile food business owes and the date by which everything must be paid. Whatever you do, don't forget to submit these payments on time lest you want Uncle Sam breathing down your neck!

Need A Little Extra Help?

If you need an extra set of hands from time to time to help with your production or sales it is possible to easily – and legally – hire temporary help. As long as any temporary employees you hire don't earn more than $599 from your business in a calendar year you can hire them and pay them with a company check but you don't have to report them to the IRS or pay employer-related taxes. Be sure to keep careful notes including a copy of all checks paid to temporary employees. This paper trail will be helpful should the IRS ever audit your company.

Health Insurance

Health Insurance. Unfortunately that's a tough nut for U.S. entrepreneurs to crack. At this point in time, as a small food entrepreneur, you are not required to offer health insurance coverage to your staff or subsidize any portion of it. Even if you don't want to purchase insurance for all of your employees you may simply want it for yourself. This is where things can get really tricky.

The best bet for personal insurance is getting on a spouse's or partner's health insurance plan as it will almost always be cheaper than getting private insurance on your own. Alternatively, if you are leaving one job to start the food truck or food cart, you may be eligible for COBRA, which would allow you to stay on your former health plan for up to 18 months. COBRA is by no means cheap, but if you have a pre-existing condition it is crucial that you remain continuously covered under some type of health insurance plan if you want any hope that future insurers will pay for any treatments related to that condition.

If you are looking for private health insurance or health insurance for employees you may want to consult a company like eHealthInsurance (www.ehealthinsurance.com) to get an understanding of what plans are available to you and get quotes for different health insurance choices. Another alternative is to contact your local homeowners or business insurance provider and see if they are affiliated with a health insurance company or if they can direct you to an agent that can tell you what options are available.

As you well know though, health insurance is a hot topic in Washington D.C. these days and all of the above could change by the time you read this. The best piece of advice is to try and stay on top of any proposed health insurance changes so you'll know how they'll impact you and any employees you hire.

Write The Business Plan

To many, the idea of writing a business plan sounds either overwhelming or just plain tedious. However, a business plan is a critical component to your business' success and will help get you started on the right foot. The business plan will help you clarify and organize all the ideas you have running through your head about the business, and it forces you to take a hard look at the finances of the business to make sure you're pricing your products in a profitable way. How detailed your plan is depends, in some ways, on whether you plan to seek funding from outside sources (see page 124 for funding options). At the very least, your business plan should include the following sections. For a sample business plan for the fictional company Sweet Bits Treat Truck, see Appendix I on page 133.

Executive Summary

If you plan on approaching an outside funding source it is wise to write a one-page summary of your business plan. Write the executive summary after you create the business plan even though it will be the first page of the plan. That way investors or bank officers can quickly read it and determine whether they want to read the rest of the plan for more information. You can think of the executive summary like a resume and if it's good enough the third party will be interested to learn more.

Business Description

This section should outline your vision for your company, a high-level view of what you plan on offering, and any guiding principles you want to incorporate into the business such as a commitment to use only all-natural or locally-sourced ingredients. Briefly include information about your existing or anticipated business format and health code certifications and requirements. This section also should include information on any risks your food business will face so you can be aware of potential issues before they happen. It's also a good idea to use this section to outline goals you have for this year and future years. Don't be afraid to reach for the sky and include some stretch goals!

Management Team

This piece is critical for a startup food business that is seeking outside funding. A good business concept without a strong management team will have a hard time getting startup capital. You must convince investors that not only is the business idea a solid one, but that you and any partners are the people who can make this happen. Highlight any experience you have that will showcase why you are the right person to run this business so that investors feel more comfortable disbursing funds to help you get your food truck up and running.

Target Market

Here is where you provide insight into who your target market is and explain what you know about them, as well as why you think your mobile food business will fit their needs.

Competition

Because you are undoubtedly not the only food truck, food cart, or even restaurant serving food in your area, include the competitive analysis you completed in Chapter 3 so that readers of the plan understand who your competition is.

Sales Channels

Use this area to outline the sales channels you plan on using to sell your products. While you don't have to specifically list where you plan to sell, it is helpful to include information about any parking permits or parking permissions you've already received. You also can use this section to expand on whether you plan to also go after other sales channels such as wholesale accounts, farmers' markets and festivals, and corporate or special events.

Marketing

You should include a brief synopsis of how you plan to market your mobile food business to customers in this section. If you have taken the time to develop a comprehensive marketing plan you may want to attach it separately to the business plan, but it's not necessary. Third parties and outside investors simply want to know that you've thought through the marketing portion of the business and that you have a plan on which you can execute. If you are talking with investors though, it's always helpful to have a written plan that you can pull out if asked rather than simply giving them a rundown of the thoughts you have off the top of your head.

Financials

Insert copies of your product cost and pricing analyses along with the associated cash forecasts. For a mobile food business that does plan to seek third-party investment, it is wise to include an income statement and balance sheet, but those are not necessary if the business will be self-funded.

A Last Word On Business Plans

A business plan should be a living document. This means that it shouldn't be something you write up once as an exercise and then forget about on your computer or toss into the back of some drawer. After you've put all this time and energy into your plan, use it to help guide you through your business decisions. Since your business plan will undoubtedly change as your business changes and market conditions flux, revisit your business plan at least once a year and update it to reflect where your business is and where you want it to go. Just like the initial stages of writing the plan, sitting down with your plan annually will help you strategize how best to grow your business.

Funding Your Mobile Dream

It seems like every time you turn around you hear another rags-to-riches entrepreneur story about someone who started out selling smoothies from a little red wagon in their neighborhood and became the city's smoothie king in a few short years. What a lot of these stories neglect to tell you is how those entrepreneurs actually managed to finance the startup and growth of their business.

First and foremost, you should complete your company's business plan and projected financials. This will give you a strong idea of how much money you'll need to get started and when you anticipate earning revenue. You will be able to approximate your business cash needs and know when there might be shortfalls. Once you know how much money you need for the initial startup costs and how long before the business starts turning a profit, the first place to look for funding is your own bank account. If you can fund part or all of your venture without a significant impact to your lifestyle it's best to start there. Self-funding enables you to keep full control and ownership of your company. And, truthfully, most bank loans and other investors won't consider putting money into your business unless they see that you are too. While it's advisable to self-fund as much of the business as possible, make sure you leave yourself a personal financial safety net for things like rent or mortgage payments, food, and other living expenses if your food truck doesn't start turning a profit as quickly as you planned.

While startup costs for a food truck, food trailer, or food cart are not as expensive as most other food businesses, they certainly aren't negligible and 100 percent self-funding may not be an option for most, in which case the following may be sources of additional capital:

Friends & Family

People who believe in you personally and in what you're trying to accomplish are your best bet for securing any additional funding you may need. Even though these are people you know well, both you and they should still approach this as a business matter. Present them with your business plan and be prepared to tell them what you will give them in exchange for their investment into your business. There are several options available.

One option is to offer friends or family who make an investment in your company is a loan repayment plan. With these loans you may be able to obtain a lower interest rate and/or more flexible repayment terms than you'd be able to secure from a bank. If you are fortunate enough to negotiate a loan with little or no interest it's important to keep in mind that the IRS will still calculate imputed interest on the loan that the lender will need to include on their tax return. The IRS uses the Applicable Federal Rate (AFR), which is set by the U.S. Treasury, to calculate the imputed interest that the lender will have to pay.

Alternatively, depending on how your company is structured, you can offer the friend or family member a percentage ownership, or equity, in the business in exchange for their investment. Remember though, this means that technically they do own a portion of the business so you want to make it clear whether this percentage of ownership entitles them to make business decisions with you or whether they're being asked to be a silent partner.

The last option available, should you have any generous friends or family with financial means, is that the IRS currently allows anyone to give money to you tax free for any purpose that you could use to fund your business. The IRS currently allows individuals to gift up to $13,000 and married couples who file jointly to gift up to $26,000 tax-free per year. If you receive a monetary gift, you are not required to report the money on your tax return as long as the money is a true gift and is not expected to be repaid at any time.

Regardless of which option you choose, remember that you will have both a personal and business/financial relationship with these people. Be sure to choose who you would like to be "partnered" with – temporarily in the case of a loan or permanently in the case of equity ownership – very carefully.

Outside Investors

Technically friends and family who make an investment in your business are considered investors, but outside investors are those who have a limited personal connection to you. Outside investors are typically either angel investors who are individuals or groups of individuals who combine their personal money into what's known as angel networks and invest it into privately held startup companies, or venture capital funds, which manage a pool of money from multiple sources with the goal of investing in businesses. In exchange for their investment in a business, both angel investors and venture capital firms usually receive equity – a portion ownership – in the company. In exchange for their investment in a business, these investors are looking for a high rate of return that will enable them to grow their investment significantly, usually within a five to seven year timeframe in order to compensate them for the risk they are taking by investing in a business without a track record or with a very limited history.

One benefit of outside investors is that you as the entrepreneur might benefit from the experience and expertise of the investor or investor group. Organizations like the angel network Zino Society (www.zinosociety.com) provides mentorship, networking opportunities, and business plan guidance to entrepreneurs. Many times angel investors or private capital firms invest in specific niche in which they that they have an area of expertise so, for example, an angel investor for your mobile food business may be an entrepreneur who got rich in the restaurant industry. These people can provide industry-specific guidance to you throughout the business process and may have valuable connections to others in the business community. At the end of the day, these investors want to see you succeed because it is their money invested in your company so most investors will try to help you as your business grows.

That doesn't mean the relationship will necessarily be easy. Not unlike a family or friend investor, a relationship with an outside investor is a business relationship first and foremost; you must feel comfortable with any investors in your business as they are part owners in the company and will be people you must work with frequently. Every investor also has a different understanding of how much control of day-to-day business operations their investment will grant them. While some may simply want quarterly business updates, others may want to be intimately involved with the running of the business. Make sure that both you and any investors have a clear understanding and agreement as to what role they will play in your business before taking any investment capital.

For a startup mobile food business the reality is that few venture capital funds will be interested in your company unless you have personal connections into those organizations. So if you are seeking outside investment, it is best to try to find angel investors. While angel investors are most commonly associated with tech startup companies, you shouldn't let the fact that you want to start a mobile food business stand in your way. In some cases, the fact that your business is different from the tech startups and has lower startup costs may work in your favor as long as you can prove why your business model is a strong one with potential to grow. The best way to find those angel investors is to start networking within your business community or to approach a local angel investing networking, like the Vermont Investor's Forum Inc.

(www.vermontinvestorsforum.com), which is a pool of angels who invest only in Vermont-based startup business.

There are a few things to know about angel investors or angel investment networks before approaching them. Each angel investor or angel network has a different protocol for how they like to be approached by entrepreneurs. Do your homework so that you know if they want you to buy a presentation slot at one of their meetings (a not uncommon practice), if you need to be introduced to the organization by one of their current members, or whether they want you to send them a copy of your business plan for review. In almost every case, you will be required to make a business presentation to explain what the money would be used for and why you are worthy of their investment. In this case a solid, well thought-out business plan with a complete set of financials and a firm understanding of how much capital is needed is an absolute must.

Bank Loans

In the current economic climate, and for the foreseeable future, getting a bank loan for your startup food truck or food cart business, including a business credit card, will be challenging, especially given that your company has no track records of sales and therefore no guarantee of success. This doesn't mean you shouldn't try for a bank loan if you need funding for your business. Be aware that bank loans and even credit card applications are more heavily scrutinized than ever before, and how well you've managed your finances and how much debt – such as student loans, car loans, mortgage, and credit cards, you're currently carrying — will make a big difference.

If you have family members who are willing and financially able to personally guarantee a bank loan, this may be another alternative. While the bank will still study your business plan, a guarantee from a financially strong guarantor, with a good credit history, provides the bank with an independent means of repayment, should the business falter or fail.

The Small Business Administration (SBA) has been tasked with trying to make more funds available to small businesses, which typically don't have ready access to traditional bank loans. The way they do this is by acting as a guarantor of the loan made through a participating financial institution. The SBA does not directly make the loan itself. While the loan application process is somewhat rigorous and you'll need to meet several SBA-required standards, an SBA loan may be the easiest way for a startup company to get funding through a bank. To learn more, visit the SBA's website at www.sba.gov, which provides a wealth of information.

If you are able to secure a bank loan, whether it's backed by the SBA or not, the contract you sign will lay out a repayment plan with interest that you'll be required to pay. Before signing a loan contract, build those loan payments into your business' financial projections to understand how the loan impacts your cash flow and if you can reasonably pay the loan back and operate your business based on the sales you anticipate.

Revolving Lines of Credit

In some cases it may be possible to apply for a line of credit from a bank but, again, with today's tightened lending practices this may be hard for a startup company to get without a strong personal credit history, collateral, and/or a guarantee from a financially strong family member.

Revolving lines of credit are not unlike a credit card that you can use as needed to cover business expenses and buy inventory. Lines of credit are made through a financial institution and are generally used to support seasonal working capital needs. The benefit of a line of credit over a bank loan is that you only pay interest on the money you actually use and stop paying interest once the money has been paid back. Additionally, a revolving line of credit can be used within its approved 12-month time period as working capital when needed to support the projected increase in sales. If you anticipate times when your business will need more cash then you can personally afford to invest —but that can be paid back within the approved 12-month term — this type of loan may be an attractive avenue to investigate.

It is important to note that banks generally like to see an "annual cleanup," or a 30- or 60-day time period when the line of credit rests at zero. This proves to the bank that the line is properly structured and is only supporting temporary or seasonal working capital needs. A permanent level of working capital should not be financed by a revolving line of credit, but is more properly supported by a medium-term bank loan, or preferably, funding through your own equity or private investors in exchange for equity.

Microlending

Traditionally only used in Third World nations as a way to provide small amounts of startup capital to small businesses and independent entrepreneurs who can't get bank loans, the recent economic upheaval and restructured lending by banks has brought this concept to North America's shores. Whereas banks traditionally prefer to only deal with loan amounts in excess of $50,000, microlending organizations disburse funds for requests that are usually less than $35,000. Like a bank, they do charge interest rates and do require that the loan be paid off in a specified timeframe. While this is still a fairly new concept to the United States, Accion USA (www.accionusa.org) is currently one of the largest microlenders to U.S. small businesses and there are approximately 400 other microlending programs around the country.

Funding Growth

As businesses grow they typically need capital or money to make that happen. If you don't initially get funding via angel investors, private equity firms or banks, you shouldn't necessarily loose all hope. As the economy has tightened in recent years, many individuals and firms are more wary of investing in startup businesses. If you have the ability to start the business with your own funds or with the help of friends or family, it is worthwhile to approach banks, angel investors, and private equity firms after you get your business off the ground. At that point you can clearly show them a track record of sales and they may be more willing to lend you money or invest in your business at that time.

The following is a sample business plan for the fictional food truck business Sweet Bits Treat Truck. This appendix is for example only and may differ from what is required for your specific mobile food business.

Sweet Bits Treat Truck

Business Plan

Tyr Smith

Founder & Chief Foodie

Address

Address

Business Phone

Business Email

Business Website

Executive Summary

Sweet Bits Treat Truck is a start-up company in Woodland that strives to be community-focused and socially and environmentally responsible while providing quality, baked-to-order gourmet dessert items. The business will initially launch with gourmet cookies and organic milk but the opportunity exists to branch into other dessert products as desired. Currently there is no other mobile food business or existing restaurant in the area that focuses on gourmet cookies.

The decision to launch with a food truck as opposed to a traditional restaurant is due to the reduced cost to acquire and outfit a food truck and the ability this gives Management to move as demand dictates. The Street Food movement is strong in Woodland with few parking restrictions which will enable Sweet Bits Food Truck to sell throughout the city as well as at area beaches, parks, festivals, and fairs, to reach a wide and varied audience.

The food truck has already been purchased. It was bought used and refurbished with the equipment needed for baking cookies and desserts quickly. The food truck also has the required three basin sink, handwash sink, and other equipment as deemed necessary by the Health Department. At this time the truck has been given its mobile health permit.

The business will rely on walk-by customers from the surrounding businesses, neighborhoods, and recreational areas as well as customers who are alerted to the truck's presence via social media. We also plan to have an aggressive advertising and public relations campaign that will reach out to our target market through defined channels. Our relationships with existing customers – along with the quality and consistently in our product – will also help generate word of mouth advertising for us via customers' own social networking sites.

Business Description

Sweet Bits Treat Truck will be a mobile food truck based in Woodland that will serve baked-to-order desserts. With a focus, initially, on gourmet cookies made from locally-sourced all-natural ingredients, Sweet Bits Treat Truck will be the only dessert-focused food truck in the area.

Management

Tyr Smith is the founder of Sweet Bits Treat Truck. Tyr's introduction to the baking world came at a young age as she helped her mother in the kitchen and, later, assisted in local bakeries as a teenager looking to make extra money. Following college, where she studied finance, Tyr took a job as a business analyst for a large consulting company but spent her nights and weekends indulging in her true passion which was baking cookies. In fact, she quickly became known in the office for the goodies she'd bring in on a regular basis. Before too long co-workers started asking Tyr to make cookies for their special occasions and, working out of her home kitchen, Tyr happily obliged. Though her consulting job provided her with excellent business skills and management experience, Tyr recently decided to follow her dream and left her position in order to get started in the cookie business.

Manager Salary Plan

Tyr will retain 95% ownership of the company and will take no more than 20% of monthly sales, not to exceed $3500 in the first three years of business, as a manager draw. Any excess monthly profit will go towards paying down the loan and ensuring that there is a healthy cash cushion for months where sales may be less than anticipated. If, after the first three years of business, the initial loan has been repaid in full, Tyr and her Board of Advisors will create a salary package for her that will still allow for investment into growing the company

Personnel

Four (4) employees will initially be hired – all staff members will have the training, experience, and required health permits to be able to bake the cookies on site as well as drive the truck and be responsible for sales.

Additional outsourced personnel include Cohen & Partners Law Firm, ABC Accounting Firm, and Tasty Graphic Design Company.

Business Licenses & Health Permits

Sweet Bits Treat Truck has received all necessary state, city, and federal business licenses and health permits and is ready to begin selling. As needed, the Company will go forward with trademark applications in the future.

Insurance

The Company is currently insured for up to $1,000,000 in damages to either property, equipment, or due to any lawsuits that may be brought against it.

Business Risks

Sweet Bits Treat Truck biggest business risk is the potential for ingredient contamination that could undermine the flavor of the products or sicken customers. To mitigate this risk, the Company has developed relationships with local ingredient purveyors where possible and, in cases where that is not economically viable, procures ingredients from reputable vendors.

Other Business Risks

There is potential for liability due to an accident involving the food truck that could injure pedestrians, other vehicles, or employees. Loss of revenue is another business risk if products do not sell as anticipated.

Current Year Business Goals

- Average monthly sales of $15,750 in peak summer season
- Create a brand that is recognizable to the core target market as is evidenced by repeat customers and customers joining in the Company's social networking efforts

Year 2 Business Goals

- $17,640 in monthly revenue – approx 12% growth from Year 1
- Win Best of Woodland Food Truck award

Year 3 Business Goals

- Repay original loan amount in full and start paying manager a guaranteed monthly salary.
- Increase average monthly sales to $20,286 to gross $243,432 annually in revenue

Customer Segmentation and Market Size

Sweet Bits Treat Truck's primary target will be families and children who congregate at area beaches, parks, and athletic events. Our handmade cookies, made with real and locally-sourced ingredients, will be the perfect treat that parents can give their children without fear of additives or preservatives. Not just for kids though, the menu will include grown-up flavors like Almond-Cardamom Twists and Drunken Chocolate-Cherry Drops.

Research indicates that there are 380,000 families with children under the age of 12, accounting for 1,330,000 million people, who live within the greater Woodland area. An online survey shared via the local zoo's blog post also indicated that 88% of parents who fall into that demographic would be willing to give their kids a locally-made treat as opposed to a mass-manufactured store-bought cookie. In fact, 79% of the parents indicated that they give treats that cost more than $3 per piece to their children regularly.

Competitive Market

Sweet Bits Treat Truck will face competition from several existing food truck establishments – two of which focus on dessert and ice cream items. However, the public has been very welcoming of food trucks in the neighborhoods and it is believed that Sweet Bits' concept will be very well received and differentiated enough from other both mobile and brick-and-mortar food businesses so as to be successful.

Sweet Bits Treat Truck
Competative Analysis

Business Name	Food Type	Mobile Y/N	Target Market	Location(s)	Comparable	Complimentary
Sweet Bits	*Gourmet Cookies*	*Y*	*children & families*	*Beaches & Parks (afternoons & evenings), Children's Sports Events, Festivals & Farmers' Markets*		
Fish Fry	Fish & Chips	Y	families, beach picnicers	Beaches & Parks	N	Y
Burger Master	Burgers & Fries	Y	college students, late-night crowd	University area	N	Y
BBQ Shack	BBQ Sandwiches	N	families, late-night crowd	6th & Pine	N	Y
Greta's Bistro	French - Full Menu	N	couples, adults	3rd & Main	Y	N
Crab Cave	Seafood - Full Menu	N	adults	7th & Keystone	Y	N
Greta's GF Goodies	Desserts	Y	children, families, adults who like dessert	Festivals, Fairs, Farmer's Markets, 4th & Market	Y	N
Dessert Haus	Desserts	N	special-order desserts	5th & Magnolia	Y	N
Ben's Ice Cream	Ice Cream	Y & N	children, families	4th & Magnolia (N), Beaches & Parks (Y), 3rd & Capital (Y)	Y	N
The Sushi Spot	Sushi - Full Menu	N	adults, couples	3rd & Pine	N	N

Alternative Distribution Strategies

The opportunity also exists for the Sweet Bits Treat Truck to be hired out for catering events such as birthday parties and special events. These events would be an additional revenue stream that is not calculated into the Year 1 financials until it is determined how popular this option is. The Company will though have marketing materials on site at all times as well as information available on the website about catering.

Sweet Bits Treat Truck is also in discussion with several family hotel chains to place their Gourmet Cookies & Milk packages within the hospitality market. The Company has targeted hotels/resorts that already have a well-known commitment to working with local businesses in order to offer their travelers the best local experience during their stay. The Gourmet Cookies & Milk packages could be part of a welcome gift during check-in or placed in the rooms as turndown treats. The wholesale price on these items would be considerably less than Sweet Bits' retail price as the Company understands that many hotels would be giving out these services at their own cost. While Sweet Bits margins in this market are smaller, the Company believes that distribution in this market will help build excitement and may help drive tourist traffic to the truck itself.

Marketing Plan

In order to best alert potential customers to the launch of the Sweet Bits Treat Truck a comprehensive marketing strategy has been developed which includes:

Social Media: The Company has already registered for a Facebook and Twitter account and has begun to build up a local following due to frequent and timely posts and tweets. In addition to

Advertising: Initially, the Company will develop targeted marketing to their demographic on Facebook and via Google Ads. These advertisements are pay-per-click with no more than $40 per month being spent on this advertising avenue.

Sponsorship: Sweet Bits Treat Truck will work with local organization, such as the youth soccer league and the neighborhood swim clubs to sponsor events in exchange for sampling or selling at events as well as being able to include promotions in those organization's e-newsletters.

Public Relations: Work has already begun to contact local newspaper, magazine, and radio reporters as well as area "motherhood" blogs that have a large parenting following.

Sweet Bits Treat Truck
Product Cost and Pricing

Chocolate Inferno Cookies
Product Cost

Ingredients	Amount Used (ounces)	Per Unit Cost	Total
gluten-free flour	5	$ 0.30	$ 1.50
cocoa powder	0.33	$ 0.13	$ 0.04
butter	8	$ 0.04	$ 0.32
eggs (per egg)	2	$ 0.15	$ 0.30
cayenne pepper	0.12	$ 0.29	$ 0.03
Total Ingredient Cost			$ 2.19
Per Piece Product Ingredient Cost (12 pieces)			$ 0.18

Packaging

Packaging	Amount Used	Per Unit Cost	Total
Labels	1	$ 0.06	$ 0.06
Takeout Box	1	$ 0.29	$ 0.29
Total Product Packaging Cost			$ 0.35

Number of Cookies per package	3
Total Per Package Ingredient Cost	$ 0.54
Total Product Cost with Packaging	$ 0.89

Product Pricing

Sales Channel	Cost	Price Charged	Profit
Individual Cookie	$ 0.18	$ 2.00	$ 1.82
Packaged Cookies	$ 0.89	$ 5.00	$ 4.11

Sweet Bits Treat Truck
Realistic Cash Forecast

	Startup	May	June	July	Aug	Sept
Fixed Costs						
Food Truck w/ Equipment	$ 60,000	$ -	$ -	$ -	$ -	$ -
Kitchen Facilities / Commissary	$ -	$ 750	$ 750	$ 750	$ 750	$ 750
Office Supplies	$ 150	$ 150	$ 150	$ 150	$ 150	$ 150
Telephone/Internet	$ 110	$ 110	$ 110	$ 110	$ 110	$ 110
Loan Repayment	$ 893	$ 893	$ 893	$ 893	$ 893	$ 893
Accounting	$ -	$ 40	$ 40	$ 40	$ 40	$ 40
Total Monthly Fixed Costs	$ 61,153	$ 1,943	$ 1,943	$ 1,943	$ 1,943	$ 1,943
Variable Costs						
Ingredients	$ -	$ 1,250	$ 1,500	$ 1,750	$ 1,750	$ 1,500
Gas	$ -	$ 347	$ 441	$ 510	$ 510	$ 441
Parking Fees	$ -	$ 125	$ 230	$ 315	$ 315	$ 230
Marketing						
Farmers' Market Minimum Fee	$ -	$ 180	$ 210	$ 240	$ 240	$ 210
Print Advertising	$ -	$ -	$ -	$ -	$ -	$ -
Online Advertising	$ -	$ 25	$ 25	$ 25	$ 25	$ 25
Newsletter/e-newsletter	$ -	$ -	$ -	$ -	$30	$ -
Marketing Postcards	$ 600	$ -	$ -	$ -	$ -	$ -
Website	$ 3,000	$ -	$ -	$ -	$ -	$ -
Photography	$ 800	$ -	$ -	$ -	$ -	$ -
Truck Wrap	$ 2,500	$ -	$ -	$ -	$ -	$ -
Total Variable Costs	$ 6,900	$ 1,927	$ 2,406	$ 2,840	$ 2,870	$ 2,406
Payroll						
Paychecks	$ -	$ 3,120	$ 3,900	$ 4,680	$ 4,680	$ 3,900
Payroll Costs	$ 200	$ 52	$ 52	$ 52	$ 52	$ 52
Payroll Taxes	$ -	$ 468	$ 585	$ 702	$ 702	$ 585
Payroll Total	$ 200	$ 3,640	$ 4,537	$ 5,434	$ 5,434	$ 4,537
Other Costs						
Packaging Costs						
Labels	$ 350	$ -	$ -	$ -	$ -	$ -
Compostable Bags	$ 200	$ -	$ -	$ -	$ -	$ -
Compostable Forks	$ 150	$ -	$ -	$ -	$ -	$ -
Business Licenses	$ 500	$ -	$ -	$ -	$ -	$ -
Health Permits	$ 650	$ -	$ -	$ -	$ -	$ -
Total Other Costs	$ 1,850	$ -	$ -	$ -	$ -	$ -
Total Operating Costs	$ 70,103	$ 7,510	$ 8,886	$ 10,217	$ 10,247	$ 8,886
Projected Sales	$ -	$ 11,250	$ 13,500	$ 15,750	$ 15,750	$ 13,500
Net Income (Sales - Costs)	$ (70,103)	$ 3,740	$ 4,614	$ 5,533	$ 5,503	$ 4,614
Starting Cash On Hand	$ 100,000	$ 29,897	$ 33,637	$ 38,251	$ 43,784	$ 49,287
+ Net Income	$ 29,897	$ 33,637	$ 38,251	$ 43,784	$ 49,287	$ 53,901
Ending Cash On Hand	$ 29,897	$ 33,637	$ 38,251	$ 43,784	$ 49,287	$ 53,901

Sweet Bits Treat Truck
Worst Case Cash Forecast

	Startup	May	June	July	Aug	Sept
Fixed Costs						
Food Truck w/ Equipment	$ 60,000	$ -	$ -	$ -	$ -	$ -
Kitchen Facilities / Commissary	$ -	$ 750	$ 750	$ 750	$ 750	$ 750
Office Supplies	$ 150	$ 150	$ 150	$ 150	$ 150	$ 150
Telephone/Internet	$ 110	$ 110	$ 110	$ 110	$ 110	$ 110
Loan Repayment	$ 893	$ 893	$ 893	$ 893	$ 893	$ 893
Accounting	$ -	$ 40	$ 40	$ 40	$ 40	$ 40
Total Monthly Fixed Costs	$ 61,153	$ 1,943	$ 1,943	$ 1,943	$ 1,943	$ 1,943
Variable Costs						
Ingredients	$ -	$ 940	$ 1,128	$ 1,316	$ 1,316	$ 1,128
Gas	$ -	$ 347	$ 405	$ 515	$ 515	$ 405
Parking Fees	$ -	$ 166	$ 222	$ 312	$ 312	$ 222
Marketing						
Farmers' Market Minimum Fee	$ -	$ 120	$ 140	$ 160	$ 160	$ 140
Print Advertising	$ -	$ -	$ -	$ -	$ -	$ -
Online Advertising	$ -	$ 25	$ 25	$ 25	$ 20	$ 20
Newsletter/e-newsletter	$ -	$ -	$ -	$ -	$30	$ -
Marketing Postcards	$ 600	$ -	$ -	$ -	$ -	$ -
Website	$ 3,000	$ -	$ -	$ -	$ -	$ -
Photography	$ 800	$ -	$ -	$ -	$ -	$ -
Truck Wrap	$ 2,500	$ -	$ -	$ -	$ -	$ -
Total Variable Costs	$ 6,900	$ 1,598	$ 1,920	$ 2,328	$ 2,353	$ 1,915
Payroll						
Paychecks	$ -	$ 1,560	$ 1,950	$ 2,340	$ 2,340	$ 1,950
Payroll Costs	$ 200	$ 52	$ 52	$ 52	$ 52	$ 52
Payroll Taxes	$ -	$ 234	$ 293	$ 351	$ 351	$ 293
Payroll Total	$ 200	$ 1,846	$ 2,295	$ 2,743	$ 2,743	$ 2,295
Other Costs						
Packaging Costs						
Labels	$ 450	$ -	$ -	$ -	$ -	$ -
Compostable Bags	$ 500	$ -	$ -	$ -	$ -	$ -
Compostable Forks	$ 500	$ -	$ -	$ -	$ -	$ -
Business Licenses	$ 500	$ -	$ -	$ -	$ -	$ -
Health Permits	$ 650	$ -	$ -	$ -	$ -	$ -
Total Other Costs	$ 2,600	$ -	$ -	$ -	$ -	$ -
Total Operating Costs	$ 70,853	$ 5,387	$ 6,157	$ 7,014	$ 7,039	$ 6,152
Projected Sales	$ -	$ 3,759	$ 4,511	$ 6,579	$ 7,895	$ 7,895
Net Income (Sales - Costs)	$ (70,853)	$ (1,628)	$ (1,646)	$ (435)	$ 856	$ 1,742
Starting Cash On Hand	$ 100,000	$ 29,147	$ 27,519	$ 25,873	$ 25,438	$ 26,294
+ Net Income	$ 29,147	$ 27,519	$ 25,873	$ 25,438	$ 26,294	$ 28,037
Ending Cash On Hand	$ 29,147	$ 27,519	$ 25,873	$ 25,438	$ 26,294	$ 28,037

Sweet Bits Treat Truck
Best Case Cash Forecast

	Startup	May	June	July	Aug	Sept
Fixed Costs						
Food Truck w/ Equipment	$ 60,000	$ -	$ -	$ -	$ -	$ -
Kitchen Facilities / Commissary	$ -	$ 750	$ 750	$ 750	$ 750	$ 750
Office Supplies	$ 150	$ 150	$ 150	$ 150	$ 150	$ 150
Telephone/Internet	$ 110	$ 110	$ 110	$ 110	$ 110	$ 110
Loan Repayment	$ 893	$ 893	$ 893	$ 893	$ 893	$ 893
Accounting	$ -	$ 40	$ 40	$ 40	$ 40	$ 40
Total Monthly Fixed Costs	**$ 61,153**	**$ 1,943**	**$ 1,943**	**$ 1,943**	**$ 1,943**	**$ 1,943**
Variable Costs						
Ingredients	$ -	$ 1,880	$ 2,256	$ 2,632	$ 2,632	$ 2,256
Gas	$ -	$ 462	$ 587	$ 678	$ 678	$ 587
Parking Fees	$ -	$ 166	$ 306	$ 419	$ 419	$ 306
Marketing						
Farmers' Market Minimum Fee	$ -	$ 240	$ 280	$ 320	$ 320	$ 280
Print Advertising	$ -	$ -	$ -	$ -	$ -	$ -
Online Advertising	$ -	$ 40	$ 40	$ 40	$ 40	$ 40
Newsletter/e-newsletter	$ -	$ -	$ -	$ -	$60	$ -
Marketing Postcards	$ 600	$ -	$ -	$ -	$ -	$ -
Website	$ 3,000	$ -	$ -	$ -	$ -	$ -
Photography	$ 800	$ -	$ -	$ -	$ -	$ -
Truck Wrap	$ 2,500	$ -	$ -	$ -	$ -	$ -
Total Variable Costs	**$ 6,900**	**$ 2,787**	**$ 3,468**	**$ 4,089**	**$ 4,149**	**$ 3,468**
Payroll						
Paychecks	$ -	$ 4,150	$ 5,187	$ 6,224	$ 6,224	$ 5,187
Payroll Costs	$ 200	$ 52	$ 52	$ 52	$ 52	$ 52
Payroll Taxes	$ -	$ 622	$ 778	$ 934	$ 934	$ 778
Payroll Total	**$ 200**	**$ 4,824**	**$ 6,017**	**$ 7,210**	**$ 7,210**	**$ 6,017**
Other Costs						
Packaging Costs						
Labels	$ 450	$ -	$ -	$ -	$ -	$ -
Compostable Bags	$ 500	$ -	$ -	$ -	$ -	$ -
Compostable Forks	$ 500	$ -	$ -	$ -	$ -	$ -
Business Licenses	$ 500	$ -	$ -	$ -	$ -	$ -
Health Permits	$ 650	$ -	$ -	$ -	$ -	$ -
Total Other Costs	**$ 2,600**	**$ -**	**$ -**	**$ -**	**$ -**	**$ -**
Total Operating Costs	**$ 70,853**	**$ 9,554**	**$ 11,428**	**$ 13,242**	**$ 13,302**	**$ 11,428**
Projected Sales	**$ -**	**$ 19,737**	**$ 23,684**	**$ 27,632**	**$ 27,632**	**$ 23,684**
Net Income (Sales - Costs)	**$ (70,853)**	**$ 10,182**	**$ 12,256**	**$ 14,390**	**$ 14,330**	**$ 12,256**
Starting Cash On Hand	**$ 100,000**	**$ 29,147**	**$ 39,329**	**$ 51,585**	**$ 65,975**	**$ 80,305**
+ Net Income	**$ 29,147**	**$ 39,329**	**$ 51,585**	**$ 65,975**	**$ 80,305**	**$ 92,561**
Ending Cash On Hand	**$ 29,147**	**$ 39,329**	**$ 51,585**	**$ 65,975**	**$ 80,305**	**$ 92,561**

Sweet Bits Treat Truck LLC
Projected Income Statement (Realistic Case)
May 1 - September 30 Year 1

	Total
Income	
Sales	69,750.00
Total Income	$ 69,750.00
Cost of Goods Sold	
Food Supplies	16,042.50
Packaging	1,350.00
Labor (Production)	23,782.00
Total Cost of Goods Sold	$ 41,174.50
Gross Profit	$ 28,575.50
Expenses	
Bank Charges	116.59
Merchant Acccount Charges	266.93
Total Bank Charges	$ 383.52
Business Licenses	59.00
Health Department Licenses	270.00
Total Business Licenses	$ 329.00
Legal & Professional Fees	
Accounting	240.00
Total Legal & Professional Fees	$ 240.00
Marketing	
Postcards/Business Cards/Collateral	1,234.87
Sponsorships/Promotions	769.36
Total Marketing	$ 2,004.23
Office Expenses	$ 201.38
Food Truck Payment	$ 3,300.00
Commissary Rent	$ 3,900.00
Labor (Administrative)	$ -
Sales Generation	
Farmers Market Booth Fees	900.00
Parking Fees	1,200.00
Total Sales Generation	$ 2,100.00
Total Expenses	$ 14,558.13
Net Income	$ 14,017.37

APPENDIX II
USEFUL CULINARY MEASUREMENTS & ABBREVIATIONS

Useful American Standard Cooking Measurements:

16 ounces	=	1 pound
1 cup	=	8 fluid ounces
8 fluid ounces	=	1 pint
16 fluid ounces	=	1 quart
64 fluid ounces	=	1 gallon

Common American Standard Measurement Abbreviations

tsp (or just t)	=	teaspoon
Tbl (or just T)	=	tablespoon
oz	=	ounces
lb	=	pound
pt	=	pint
qt	=	quart
gal	=	gallon

APPENDIX III
RECIPE TESTING WORKSHEET

Recipe Name
# of Servings
Date:

Weight	Ingredient

Instructions

Storage Requirements

Comments/Feedback

APPENDIX IV
COMPETATIVE ANALYSIS WORKSHEET

Competative Analysis

Business Name	Food Type	Mobile Y/N	Target Market	Location(s)	Comparable	Complimentary	Differentiation

PRODUCT COST WORKSHEET

[Company Name]
Product Cost

[Product Name]

Step 1A: Ingredient Unit Cost

Ingredients	Total Units Bought (total weight)	Total Price	Unit Cost

Divide Total Price by Total Units Bought to get Unit Cost

Step 1B: Product Ingredient Cost

Ingredient	Amount Used	Unit Cost	Ingredient Unit Cost

Multiply Amount Used by Unit Cost to get Ingredient Unit Cost

Step 1C: Total Ingredient Cost

Total Ingredient Cost	

Add all Ingredient Unit Costs together

Step 1D: Per Piece Ingredient Cost

Total Ingredient Cost	Number of Units Recipe Yields	Per Piece Ingredient Cost

Divide Total Ingredient Cost by Number of Units Recipe Yields

Step 2: Packaging Unit Cost

Packaging	Total Amount Bought	Total Price	Unit Cost

Divide Total Price by Total Amount Bought to get Unit Cost

Total Packaging Cost			

Mutiply each Unit Cost by the number of units used per sale

Step 3: Total Product Cost

Total Ingredient Cost (Ingredient Cost x number of products per package)	
Add in Total Packaging Cost	
Total Product Cost	

[Company Name]
Product Pricing

[Product Name]
Total Product Cost: (from Product Cost Worksheet)

Step 1: Base Price

Wholesale Price	(Total Product Cost x 2)

Retail Price	(Total Product Cost x 4)

Step 2: Adjusted Price

Adjusted Wholesale Price

Adjusted Retail Price

Adjust the price accordingly to account for specific market conditions and if product is especially time consuming.
This will be the price you sell your products for.

Step 3: Gross Profit
Gross Profit shows you how much money you will make on each product sale after you account for the costs associated with that product

Wholesale Gross Profit

Subtract the Total Product Cost from the Adjusted Wholesale Price to calculate your Wholesale Profit

Retail Gross Profit

Subtract the Total Product Cost from the Adjusted Retail Price to calculate your Wholesale Profit

Step 4: Markup
Markup is the percentage difference between the Total Product Cost and the Adjusted Wholesale/Retail Price. In some instances you may decide that you want to price a product based on the markup you would receive.

Step 4a: Calculating Markup with Price in Place

Wholesale Markup

Divide Wholesale Gross Profit by the Total Product Cost

Retail Markup

Divide Retail Gross Profit by the Total Product Cost

Step 4b: Calculating Price Based on Desired Markup
Markup Percentage You Want

Subtract Markup Percentage (in decimal form) from 1
ie - 60% = .6 = 1-.6 = .4

Divide Total Product Cost by 1-markup percentage
for Wholesale Price

Reminder - your Wholesale Markup and Retail Markup will be different from one another and should be calculated seperately

Step 5: Margin
Margin is the percentage difference between the Adjusted Price and the Gross Profit

Wholesale Margin

Divide Wholesale Gross Profit by Adjusted Wholesale Price

Retail Margin

Divide Retail Gross Profit by Adjusted Retail Price

APPENDIX VII
GAS PRICE WORKSHEET

[Company Name]
Gas Price Worksheet

Input the following information:
Number of Miles Per Gallon:_____

Number of Gallons Per Tank:_____

Avg Miles Driven Daily:_____

Number of Days Per Month Worked: _____

Average Area Gas Price: _____

Current Monthly Gas Cost:
_____ (cost per gallon) / _____(miles per gallon) = _____ (gas cost per mile)

_____(gas cost per mile) x _____(miles driven per day) = _____ (daily gas cost)

_____ (daily gas cost) x _____(days worked per month) = _____ (Monthly Gas Cost)

To understand how increases or decreases in gas prices will impact your mobile food business, repeat the formula with different gas price figures:

Estimated Monthly Gas Cost:
_____ (est. cost per gallon) / _____(miles per gallon) = _____ (est. gas cost per mile)

_____(est. gas cost per mile) x _____(miles driven per day) = _____ (est. daily gas cost)

_____ (est. daily gas cost) x _____(days worked per month) = _____ (New Monthly Gas Cost)

APPENDIX VIII

CASH FORECAST WORKSHEET

Company Name
[Best/Realistic/Worst] Cash Forecast

Month:

Fixed Costs

Kitchen Facilities						
Office Supplies						
Telephone/Internet						
Accounting						
Website						
Add Each Month's Fixed Costs						

Variable Costs

Ingredients						
Marketing						
Add Each Month's Variable Costs						

Other Costs

Packaging Costs						
Add Each Month's Other Costs						

Add Fixed, Variable, & Other Costs						

Projected Sales						

Net Income (Sales - Costs)						

Starting Cash On Hand						
+ Net Income						
Net Income = Ending Cash						

PROJECTED INCOME STATEMENT WORKSHEET

Your projected Income Statement line items may vary depending on the specifics of your business.

Company Name
Projected Income Statement
Date & Year

	Total
Income	
Sales	All anticipated sales (price times quantity)
Other Income	May include shipping fees, delivery fees, etc. for which you are paid
Total Income	**Add together above amounts**
Cost of Goods Sold	
Food Supplies	All anticipated ingredient costs
Packaging	All anticipated packaging costs
Labor (Production)	All labor costs attributable to cooking or packaging
Total Cost of Goods Sold	**Add together Food, Packaging, and Production Labor costs**
Gross Profit	**Total Income - Total Cost of Goods Sold**
Expenses	
Bank Charges	All anticipated bank fees except merchant or other misc fees
Merchant Acccount Charges	All anticipated merchant account fees
Other Bank Charges	All other anticipated bank fees
Total Bank Charges	**Add together all Bank, Merchant, and Other charges**
Business Licenses	All anticipated business licensing costs
Health Department Licenses	Health Department and Food Handlers fees as applicable
Total Business Licenses	**Add together all Business Licensing and Health Fees**
Legal & Professional Fees	
Accounting	All anticipated accountant, bookkeeper, or software program costs
Legal Fees	Any anticipated attorney costs
Total Legal & Professional Fees	**Add together Legal & Professional Fees**
Marketing	
Postcards/Business Cards/Collateral	Estimated or budgeted marketing collateral costs
Print Marketing	Estimated or budgeted print marketing costs
EMarketing	Estimated or budgeted eMarketing costs
Total Marketing	**Add together all Marketing expenses**
Office Expenses	May include phone, paper, etc
Rent or Lease	Kitchen rent and any other leased property or equipment
Labor (Administrative)	All labor costs not directly attributable to production
Sales Generation	Estimated expenditure will depend on sales channel
Total Expenses	**Total Sales Generation + Labor + Rent + Office + Marketing + Legal/Professional + Licenses + Bank Fees**
Net Operating Income	**Gross Profit - Total Expenses**

APPENDIX X
PROJECTED BALANCE SHEET WORKSHEET

Your projected Balance Sheet line items may vary depending on the specifics of your business.

Company name
Projected Balance Sheet
Date Year 1

	Total
ASSETS	
Current Assets	
Bank Accounts	Taken from Realistic Cash Forecast
Accounts Receivable	Anticipated outstanding revenue from sales not yet collected
Other Current Assets	
Inventory	Anticipated remaining food or packaging inventory
Total Current Assets	**Add together all Current Assets**
Fixed Assets	
Property/Equipement/Vehicles	Value of Fixed Assets minus accumulated depreciation
Total Fixed Assets	**Add together all Fixed Assets**
TOTAL ASSETS	**Sum of all Current and Fixed Assets**
LIABILITIES AND EQUITY	
Liabilities	
Current Liabilities	List all anticipated current liabilities - ie credit cards
Other Current Liabilities	List all other current liabilities such as taxes and loans
Total Current Liabilities	**Add together all Current and Other Current Liabilities**
Long-Term Liabilities	List all anticipated Long Term Liabilities like bank notes payable
Total Long-Term Liabilities	**Add together all Long-Term Liabilities**
TOTAL LIABILITIES	**Sum of Current Liabilities and any Long-Term Liabilities**
EQUITY	
Owner's Equity	Add together investments made into the business by Owner 1
Add more lines for additional Owners	
Net Income/Loss	**Taken from Projected Income Statement**
TOTAL EQUITY	**All Partners' Equity + Retained Earnings + Net Income/Loss**
TOTAL LIABILITIES AND EQUITY	**Total Liabilities + Total Equity**

Total Liabilities and Equity must equal Total Assets

APPENDIX XI
CULINARY RESOURCES

While by no means a comprehensive list, the following section provides respected resources for some of your culinary needs.

Ingredient Suppliers

When starting out, especially while testing recipes, it may be easiest to simply purchase ingredients at your local grocery store or supermarket. Don't forget to check with local farmers who may be willing to offer wholesale prices on their ingredients to food businesses. For ingredients you can't source locally or for larger quantities several options include:

Costco® - A membership warehouse store that sells ingredients in larger quantity sizes at a discount over local grocery stores and supermarkets. (costco.com)

GloryBee Foods® - What started as a honey company has turned into a purveyor of natural foods. Call to set up a wholesale account in order to take advantage of their bulk pricing. (glorybeefoods.com)

Peterson® - While based in the Northwest with a focus on serving Northwest companies, Peterson does sell and distribute its specialty food items such as imported cheeses and hard-to-find baking and cooking ingredients nationwide. (petersoncheese.com)

Sam's Club® – Another membership warehouse store selling ingredients in larger quantity sizes. (samsclub.com)

United Natural Foods, Inc® – A respected distributor of natural and organic ingredients, produce and culinary products. You will need to set up a wholesale account before placing orders. (unfi.com)

Packaging Suppliers

Local cake and craft stores are a great place to purchase small quantities of packaging supplies. When you're ready for larger quantities of packaging the following companies offer a wide range of options and several can do custom work as needed. Keep in mind that food packaging must meet FDA requirements for direct food contact.

Bags & Bows® - This company mainly focuses on packaging products retailers need such as shopping bags and tissue paper but also has a wide range of ribbons and shipping supplies. (bagsandbowsonline.com)

Brpboxshop® - For bakery businesses specifically, this company has numerous packaging options including several eco-friendly choices. (brpboxshop.com)

GlerupRevere Packaging® - Whether you're looking for attractive boxes, candy pads, or custom-designed labels, GlerupRevere offers just about anything a small food business needs to get started. (glerup.com)

Label Impressions® - This California based company produces a line of eco-friendly labels and can do print runs as low as 500 labels though greater discounts do apply for larger quantity orders. (labelimpressions.com)

Nashville Wraps® - This company has an extensive line of gift and food packaging products whether you're looking for ribbons, bags, or beautiful boxes. Low order minimums make this a great option for small food entrepreneurs. (nashvillewraps.com)

Papermart® - With an extensive range of products – everything from bags to boxes to ribbons to bows – this company is a great resource for small food businesses and offers very competitive prices and low minimum orders. (papermart.com)

Uline® - If you need shipping supplies such as cardboard shipping boxes or packing material, Uline is one of the largest online retailers with prices that are significantly cheaper then you will find at your local shipping store. (uline.com)

Vegware™ - A maker of compostable and biodegradable plates, bowls, cups, cutlery, etc. They have a wide range of products for any mobile food vendor who wants a more eco-friendly option.

Kitchen Equipment

Many cities have restaurant supply stores or even a section of the city known as 'restaurant row' where you will be able to find commercial restaurant equipment at prices lower than typical kitchen retail stores. Also be sure to keep an eye on Craigslist® where good deals can be found on used kitchen equipment. You may also want to check out your local Target®, Kmart®, or other large retailer. Depending on what piece of equipment or cooking utensil you're looking for, their prices can be very competitive. Some other places to check include:

Chef's Catalog® - Based in Colorado, Chef's Catalog is a print and online catalog mainly focused on home cooks with a wide range of cooking and baking supplies. (chefscatalog.com)

Sur La Table® - The focus of this company is to provide everything home cooks need including appliances, cookbooks, and even culinary classes. (surlatable.com)

Williams Sonoma® - Undoubtedly the powerhouse in the culinary equipment world, Williams Sonoma offers thousands of products from around the world online and in their stores. (williams-sonoma.com)

Wilton® - This company focuses on kitchen equipment for baked goods such as cake pans, piping bags, and piping tips. Many of their products can be found in craft stores or through their online store. (wilton.com)

APPENDIX XII
MOBILE FOOD UNIT RESOURCES

The following is a partial list of places where you can purchase or lease food trucks, food kiosks, food trailers, and food carts. Some of these companies may also be able to help you understand and meet health regulations in your area.

All A Cart Manufacturing – allacart.com

Apollo Carts – apollocarts.com

Armenco Cater Truck Mfg. Co – cateringtruck.com

Cart Concepts International – cartconcept.com

Concession Trailers Warehouse – concessiontrailerswarehouse.com

Food Cart USA – foodcartusa.com

Mobi Munch – mobimunch.com/leasing

NW Mobile Kitchens – northwestmobilekitchens.com

Road Stoves – roadstoves.com

Vending Trucks – vendingtrucks.com

APPENDIX XIII
BUSINESS RESOURCES

The following is a list of business resources and websites that have been mentioned throughout this book.

Accion USA – accionusa.org

Applicable Federal Rate – irs.gov/app/picklist/list/federalrates.html

Blogger – blogger.com

Community Kitchen For Rent – commercialkitchenforrent.com

CompuFood Analysis, Inc – compufoodanalysis.com

Constant Contact – constantcontact.com

CostCo – costco.com

Craigslist – craigslist.com

Daily Gourmet – dailygourmet.com

eLance – elance.com

Facebook – facebook.com

Facebook Ads – facebook.com/ads

Foodzie – foodzie.com

FourSquare – foursquare.com

GasBuddy – gasbuddy.com

Google Adwords – google.com/adwords

Google Analytics – google.com/analytics

Gowalla – gowalla.com

Graphic Designers Freelance – graphicdesigners.freelancers.com

Help A Reporter Out – helpareporter.com

HubSpot – hubspot.com

i Freelance – ifreelance.com

Internal Revenue Service – irs.gov

Intuit – intuit.com

MailChimp – mailchimp.com

NASFT Fancy Food Shows – specialtyfood.com

Neighborhood Scout – neighborhoodscout.com

PayPal – paypal.com

QuickBooks – quickbooks.intuit.com

Quicken – quicken.intuit.com

Square Credit Card Processing – squareup.com

Squarespace – squarespace.com

Twitter – twitter.com

Twitter Search – twitter.com/#!/search-home

US Census Report – census.gov

US Patent and Trademark Office – uspto.gov

US Small Business Administration – sba.gov

Vermont Investor's Forum – vermontinvestorsforum.com

WordPress – wordpress.com

Zino Society – zinosociety.com

Yelp – yelp.com

APPENDIX XIV
BUSINESS STARTUP CHECKLIST

___ Build Business Plan
    ___ Business description (company description, who is your target market, who are the competitors)
    ___ Recipe testing & product cost analysis
    ___ Finalize product portfolio and pricing
    ___ Complete projected cash forecasts and financial models
    ___ Determine business structure (with legal counsel as needed)
    ___ Decide on Business Name
    ___ Outline best sales channels
    ___ Create marketing and branding strategy
___ Begin identifying outside funding sources (as needed)
___ Begin searching for food truck, food trailer, or food cart
___ Begin researching ideal selling locations and parking restrictions
___ Find kitchen space or commissary as needed
___ Register business with state authorities
___ Register business with city or county (as needed)
___ Sign up for Employer Identification Number (as needed)
___ Register with state tax authorities
___ Pass Food Handler's Safety exam (as needed)
___ Register business with local Health authorities (as needed)
___ Open business bank accounts
___ Finalize outside funding (as needed)
___ Purchase or lease mobile food unit if you have not yet done so
___ Develop brand logo, website, and other marketing collateral
___ Create wrap for mobile food unit
___ Purchase and familiarize yourself with accounting software
___ Register for merchant account (as needed)
___ Create Twitter, Facebook, and other social media logins and start building an audience
___ Start selling!
___ Keep accounting books up to date
___ Regularly update business plan to reflect actual sales experience

APPENDIX XV
STATE AND US TERRITORY STARTUP ROADMAP

Each state and US territory provides information online about how to open a small business in that region. The following pages provide links to those government resources to help get you started. Since the rules and guidelines for each state and US territory differ from one another, please take some time to thoroughly review the information. When in doubt, consult with an experienced business attorney or small business administration official.

IRS Employer Identification Number (EIN) irs.gov/businesses/small/index.html

Alabama
Alabama State Website	alabama.gov
Information on Starting a Business	alabama.gov/portal/secondary.jsp?page=Business
Business Structure Filing	sos.state.al.us/BusinessServices/Default.aspx
Business Name Registration	Not necessary but can be done through Secretary of State
City or County Buiness Licensing	Contact your city or county revenue department
Business Tax Registration	ador.state.al.us/bus.html
Health Code Requirements and Permits	Contact your city or county health department
Small Business Administration Office	sba.gov/localresources/district/al/index.html

Alaska
Alaska State Website	alaska.gov
Information on Starting a Business	alaska.gov/businessHome.html
Business Structure Filing	commerce.state.ak.us/occ/cforms.htm
Business Name Registration	commerce.state.ak.us/occ/register.html
Business Tax Registration	tax.alaska.gov
Health Code Rquirements and Permits	Contact you city or county health department
Small Business Administration Office	sba.gov/localresources/district/ak/index.html

Arizona
Arizona State Website	az.gov
Information on Starting a Business	azcommerce.com/BusAsst/SmallBiz/
Business Structure Filing	azcc.gov/divisions/corporations/filings/forms/index.htm
Business Name Registration	Not necessary but can be done through Secretary of State
Business Tax Registration	aztaxes.gov
City or County Business Licenses	Contact your city or county revenue department
Health Code Requirements and Permits	Contact your city or county health department
Small Business Administration Office	sba.gov/localresources/district/ar/index.html

Arkansas
Arkansas State Website	portal.arkansas.gov
Information on Starting a Business	portal.arkansas.gov/business/Pages/default.aspx
Business Structure Filing	sos.arkansas.gov/corp_ucc_business.html
Business Name Registration	sos.arkansas.gov/corp_ucc_business.html
Business Tax Registration	dfa.arkansas.gov/offices/incomeTax/Pages/default.aspx
City or County Business Licenses	Contact you city or county health department
Health Code Requirements and Permits	Contact your city or county health department
Small Business Administration Office	sba.gov/localresources/district/ar/index.html

California

CaliforniaState Website	ca.gov
Information on Starting a Business	calbusiness.ca.gov
Business Structure Filing	sos.ca.gov/business/be/forms.htm
Business Name Registration	Contact your County Recorder Clerk's Office
Business Tax Registration	taxes.ca.gov
City or County Business Licenses	Contact your city or county revenue department
Health Code Requirements and Permits	Contact your city or county health department
Small Business Administration Office	sba.gov/localresources/district/ca/

Colorado

Colorado State Website	colorado.gov
Information on Starting a Business	colorado.gov
Business Structure Filing	sos.state.co.us/pubs/business/main.htm
Business Name Registration	sos.state.co.us/biz/FileDoc.do
Business Tax Registration	colorado.gov/revenue/tax
City or County Business Licenses	Contact your city or county revenue department
Health Code Requirements and Permits	Contact your city or county health department
Small Business Administration Office	sba.gov/localresources/district/co/index.html

Connecticut

Connecticut State Website	ct.gov
Information on Starting a Business	ct.gov/ctportal/taxonomy/taxonomy.asp?DLN=27187&ctportalNav=|27187|
Business Structure Filing	ct.gov/sots/site/default.asp
Business Name Registration	ct.gov/sots/site/default.asp
Business Tax Registration	ct.gov/drs/cwp/view.asp?a=1433&q=265880
City or County Business Licenses	Contact your city or county revenue department
Health Code Requirements and Permits	Contact your city or county health department
Small Business Administration Office	sba.gov/localresources/district/ct/index.html

Delaware

Delaware State Website	delaware.gov
Information on Starting a Business	dedo.delaware.gov
Business Structure Filing	corp.delaware.gov/howtoform.shtml
Business Name Registration	Depends on business structure
Business Tax Registration	onestop.delaware.gov/osbrlpublic/Home.jsp
City or County Business Licenses	Contact your city or county revenue department
Health Code Requirements and Permits	Contact your city or county health department
Small Business Administration Office	sba.gov/localresources/district/de/index.html

District of Columbia

District of Columbia Website	dc.gov
Information on Starting a Business	brc.dc.gov
Business Structure Filing	dcra.dc.gov/DC/DCRA/
Business Name Registration	dcra.dc.gov/DC/DCRA/
Business Tax Registration	taxpayerservicecenter.com/fr500/
Health Code Requirements and Permits	dchealth.dc.gov
Small Business Administration Office	sba.gov/localresources/district/dc/index.html

Florida

Florida State Website	myflorida.com
Information on Starting a Business	myflorida.com/taxonomy/business/
Business Structure Filing	sunbiz.org
Business Name Registration	efile.sunbiz.org/ficregintro.html
Business Tax Registration	dor.myflorida.com/dor/taxes/registration.html
City or County Business Licenses	Contact your city or county revenue department
Health Code Requirements and Permits	Contact your city or county health department
Small Business Administration Office	sba.gov/localresources/district/fl/

Georgia

Georgia State Website	georgia.gov
Information on Starting a Business	georgia.gov/00/channel_title/0,2094,4802_4971,00.html
Business Structure Filing	sos.georgia.gov/corporations/
Business Name Registration	Depends on business structure
Business Tax Registration	etax.dor.ga.gov/ctr/formsreg.aspx
City or County Business Licenses	Contact your city or county revenue department
Health Code Requirements and Permits	Contact your city or county health department
Small Business Administration Office	sba.gov/localresources/district/ga/index.html

Guam

Guam Government Website	guam.gov
Information on Starting a Business	investguam.com
Business Structure Filing	govguamdocs.com/revtax/index_revtax.htm
Business Name Registration	guamcourts.org/CompilerofLaws/GCA/18gca/18gc026.PDF
Business Tax Registration	guamtax.com/
City or County Business Licenses	Contact your city or county revenue department
Health Code Requirements and Permits	Contact Department of Health fo rmore information
Small Business Administration Office	sba.gov/localresources/district/gu/index.html

Hawaii

Hawaii State Website	hawaii.gov
Information on Starting a Business	hbe.ehawaii.gov/BizEx/home.eb
Business Structure Filing	hbe.ehawaii.gov/BizEx/home.eb
Business License Registration	hbe.ehawaii.gov/BizEx/home.eb
Business Name Registration	hbe.ehawaii.gov/BizEx/home.eb
Business Tax Registration	hbe.ehawaii.gov/BizEx/home.eb
City or County Business Licenses	Contact your city or county revenue department
Health Code Requirements and Permits	Contact your city or county health department
Small Business Administration Office	sba.gov/localresources/district/hi/index.html

Idaho

Idaho State Website	idaho.gov
Information on Starting a Business	business.idaho.gov
Business Structure Filing	sos.idaho.gov/corp/corindex.htm
Business Name Registration	sos.idaho.gov/corp/ABNform.htm
Business Tax Registration	labor.idaho.gov/applications/ibrs/ibr.aspx
City or County Business Licenses	Contact your city or county revenue department
Health Code Requirements and Permits	Contact your city or county health department
Small Business Administration Office	sba.gov/localresources/district/id/index.html

Illinois

Illinois State Website	illinois.gov
Information on Starting a Business	business.illinois.gov
Business Structure Filing	business.illinois.gov/registration.cfm
Business Name Registration	Depends on structure - cyberdriveillinois.com/
Business Tax Registration	business.illinois.gov/registration.cfm
City or County Business Licenses	Contact your city or county health department
Health Code Requirements and Permits	Contact your city or county health department
Small Business Administration Office	sba.gov/localresources/district/il/index.html

Indiana

Indiana State Website	in.gov
Information on Starting a Business	in.gov/ai/business
Business Structure Filing	in.gov/sos/business/2381.htm
Business Name Registration	File with County Recorder and in.gov/sos/business/2436.htm
Business Tax Registration	in.gov/dor/3963.htm
City or County Business Licenses	Contact your city or county revenue department
Health Code Requirements and Permits	Contact your city or county health department
Small Business Administration Office	sba.gov/localresources/district/in/index.html

Iowa

Iowa State Website	iowa.gov
Information on Starting a Business	iowa.gov/Business_and_Economic_Development
Business Structure Filing	sos.state.ia.us/business/
Business Name Registration	Either County Recorder or sos.state.ia.us/business/index.html
Business Tax Registration	idr.iowa.gov/CBA/start.asp
City or County Business Licenses	Contact your city or county revenue department
Health Code Requirements and Permits	Contact your city or county health department
Small Business Administration Office	sba.gov/localresources/district/ia

Kansas

Kansas State Website	kansas.gov
Information on Starting a Business	kansas.gov/business
Business Structure Filing	kssos.org/
Business Name Registration	kssos.org/
Business Tax Registration	ksrevenue.org/busregistration.htm
City or County Business Licenses	Contact your city or county revenue department
Health Code Requirements and Permits	Contact your city or county health department
Small Business Administration Office	sba.gov/localresources/district/ks

Kentucky

Kentucky State Website	kentucky.gov
Information on Starting a Business	kentucky.gov/business
Business Structure Filing	sos.ky.gov/business/filings/
Business Name Registration	sos.ky.gov/business/filings/
Business Tax Registration	revenue.ky.gov/business/register.htm
City or County Business Licenses	Contact your city or county revenue department
Health Code Requirements and Permits	Contact your city or county health department
Small Business Administration Office	sba.gov/localresources/district/ky/index.html

Louisiana

Louisiana State Website	louisiana.gov
Information on Starting a Business	louisiana.gov/business
Business Structure Filing	sos.louisiana.gov
Business Name Registration	Either Parish Clerk or sos.louisiana.gov
Business Tax Registration	revenue.louisiana.gov/sections/business/intro.aspx
City or County Business Licenses	Contact your city or county revenue department
Health Code Requirements and Permits	Contact your city or county health department
Small Business Administration Office	sba.gov/localresources/district/la/index.html

Maine

Maine State Website	maine.gov
Information on Starting a Business	maine.gov/portal/business/
Business Structure Filing	maine.gov/sos/cec/corp/index/html
Business Name Registration	maine.gov/sos/cec/corp/index/html
Business Tax Registration	https://www.maine.gov/online/suwtaxreg/
City or County Business Licenses	Contact your city or county revenue department
Health Code Requirements and Permits	Contact your city or county health department
Small Business Administration Office	sba.gov/localresources/district/me/index.html

Maryland

Maryland State Website	maryland.gov
Information on Starting a Business	dat.state.md.us/sdatweb/checklist.html
Business Structure Filing	dat.state.md.us/sdatweb/sdatforms.html#entity
Business Name Registration	dat.state.md.us/sdatweb/nameappl.pdf
Business Tax Registration	interactive.marylandtaxes.com/webapps/comptrollercra/entrance.asp
City or County Business Licenses	Contact your city or county revenue department
Health Code Requirements and Permits	Contact your city or county health department
Small Business Administration Office	sba.gov/localresources/district/md/index.html

Massachusetts

Massachusetts State Website	mass.gov
Information on Starting a Business	mass.gov
Business Structure Filing	sec.state.ma.us/cor/coridx.htm
Business Name Registration	Register with city or town you are doing business in
Business Tax Registration	mass.gov/?pageID=dorhomepage&L=1&L0=Home&sid=Ador
City or County Business Licenses	Contact your city or county revenue department
Health Code Requirements and Permits	Contact your city or county health department
Small Business Administration Office	sba.gov/localresources/district/ma/index.html

Michigan

Michigan State Website	michigan.gov
Information on Starting a Business	michigan.gov/som/0,1607,7-192-29943---,00.html
Business Structure Filing	michigan.gov/som/0,1607,7-192-29943---,00.html
Business Name Registration	Depends on business structure - michigan.gov/sos
Business Tax Registration	michigan.gov/uia/0,1607,7-118--89978--,00.html
City or County Business Licenses	Contact your city or county revenue department
Health Code Requirements and Permits	Contact your city or county health department
Small Business Administration Office	sba.gov/localresources/district/mi/index.html

Minnesota

Minnesota State Website	state.mn.us
Information on Starting a Business	state.mn.us
Business Structure Filing	sos.state.mn.us/index.aspx?page=18
Business Name Registration	sos.state.mn.us/index.aspx?page=180
Business Tax Registration	mndor.state.mn.us/tp/MN_xwTapReg.aspx
City or County Business Licenses	Contact your city or county revenue department
Health Code Requirements and Permits	Contact your city or county health department
Small Business Administration Office	sba.gov/localresources/district/mn/index.html

Mississippi

Mississippi State Website	mississippi.gov
Information on Starting a Business	ms.gov/ms_sub_template.jsp?Category_ID=3
Business Structure Filing	sos.ms.gov/business_services_business_formation.aspx
Business Name Registration	Not required to register business name
Business Tax Registration	tax.ms.gov/regist.html
City or County Business Licenses	Contact your city or county revenue department
Health Code Requirements and Permits	Contact your city or county health department
Small Business Administration Office	sba.gov/localresources/district/ms/index.html

Missouri

Missouri State Website	mo.gov
Information on Starting a Business	business.mo.gov/
Business Structure Filing	sos.mo.gov/business/corporations/startBusiness.asp
Business Name Registration	sos.mo.gov
Business Tax Registration	dor.mo.gov/business/register/
City or County Business Licenses	Contact your city or county revenue department
Health Code Requirements and Permits	Contact your city or county health department
Small Business Administration Office	sba.gov/localresources/district/mo/

Montana

Montana State Website	mt.gov
Information on Starting a Business	mt.gov/business.asp
Business Structure Filing	sos.mt.gov/Business/index.asp
Business Name Registration	sos.mt.gov/Business/index.asp
Business Tax Registration	app.mt.gov/bustax/
City or County Business Licenses	Contact your city or county revenue department
Health Code Requirements and Permits	Contact your city or county health department
Small Business Administration Office	sba.gov/localresources/district/mt/index.html

Nebraska

Nebraska State Website	nebraska.gov
Information on Starting a Business	nebraska.gov/dynamicindex.html#
Business Structure Filing	sos.ne.gov/business/corp_serv/corp_stat_menu.html
Business Name Registration	sos.ne.gov
Business Tax Registration	revenue.state.ne.us/business/bus_regist.html
City or County Business Licenses	Contact your city or county revenue department
Health Code Requirements and Permits	Contact your city or county health department
Small Business Administration Office	sba.gov/localresources/district/ne/index.html

Nevada

Nevada State Website	nv.gov
Information on Starting a Business	nv.gov/NV_default4.aspx?id=182
Business Structure Filing	nvsos.gov/index.aspx?page=415
Business Name Registration	File with County Clerk
Business Tax Registration	nevadatax.nv.gov/WEB/default.aspx
City or County Business Licenses	Contact your city or county revenue department
Health Code Requirements and Permits	Contact your city or county health department
Small Business Administration Office	sba.gov/localresources/district/nv/index.html

New Hampshire

New Hampshire State Website	nh.gov
Information on Starting a Business	nh.gov/business/
Business Structure Filing	http://www.sos.nh.gov/corporate/
Business Name Registration	sos.nh.gov/corporate/tradenameforms.html
Business Tax Registration	nh.gov/revenue/faq/gti-rev.htm
City or County Business Licenses	Contact your city or county revenue department
Health Code Requirements and Permits	Contact your city or county health department
Small Business Administration Office	sba.gov/localresources/district/nh/index.html

New Jersey

New Jersey State Website	state.nj.us
Information on Starting a Business	nj.gov/njbusiness/
Business Structure Filing	state.nj.us/treasury/revenue/dcr/filing/leadpg.htm
Business Name Registration	Register with County Clerk
Business Tax Registration	state.nj.us/treasury/revenue/dcr/filing/leadpg.htm
City or County Business Licenses	Contact your city or county revenue department
Health Code Requirements and Permits	Contact your city or county health department
Small Business Administration Office	sba.gov/localresources/district/nj/index.html

New Mexico

New Mexico State Website	newmexico.gov
Information on Starting a Business	newmexico.gov/business.php
Business Structure Filing	nmprc.state.nm.us/cb.htm
Business Name Registration	Not required in New Mexico
Business Tax Registration	tax.newmexico.gov/Businesses/Pages/Home.aspx
City or County Business Licenses	Contact your city or county revenue department
Health Code Requirements and Permits	Contact your city or county health department
Small Business Administration Office	sba.gov/localresources/district/nm/index.html

New York

New York State Website	state.ny.us
Information on Starting a Business	nysegov.com/citGuide.cfm?superCat=28
Business Structure Filing	nysegov.com/citGuide.cfm?superCat=28
Business Name Registration	Depends on business structure
Business Tax Registration	tax.state.ny.us/
City or County Business Licenses	Contact your city or county revenue department
Health Code Requirements and Permits	Contact your city or county health department
Small Business Administration Office	sba.gov/localresources/district/ny/

North Carolina

North Carolina State Website	ncgov.com
Information on Starting a Business	nccommerce.com/en/BusinessServices/StartYourBusiness/
Business Structure Filing	secretary.state.nc.us/corporations/
Business Name Registration	nccommerce.com/en/BusinessServices/StartYourBusiness/
Business Tax Registration	dornc.com/forms/index.html
City or County Business Licenses	Contact your city or county revenue department
Health Code Requirements and Permits	Contact your city or county health department
Small Business Administration Office	sba.gov/localresources/district/nc/index.html

North Dakota

North Dakota State Website	nd.gov
Information on Starting a Business	nd.gov/category.htm?id=69
Business Structure Filing	nd.gov/sos/businessserv
Business Name Registration	nd.gov/sos/businessserv/registrations/tradename.html
Business Tax Registration	nd.gov/businessreg
City or County Business Licenses	Contact your city or county revenue department
Health Code Requirements and Permits	Contact your city or county health department
Small Business Administration Office	sba.gov/localresources/district/nd/index.html

Ohio

Ohio State Website	ohio.gov
Information on Starting a Business	business.ohio.gov
Business Structure Filing	sos.state.oh.us/SOS/businessServices.aspx
Business Name Registration	sos.state.oh.us
Business Tax Registration	business.ohio.gov/efiling/
City or County Business Licenses	Contact your city or county revenue department
Health Code Requirements and Permits	Contact your city or county health department
Small Business Administration Office	sba.gov/localresources/district/oh/columbus/index.html

Oklahoma

Oklahoma State Website	ok.gov
Information on Starting a Business	ok.gov/section.php?sec_id=4
Business Structure Filing	sos.ok.gov/business/
Business Name Registration	sos.ok.gov/
Business Tax Registration	tax.ok.gov/
City or County Business Licenses	Contact your city or county revenue department
Health Code Requirements and Permits	Contact your city or county health department
Small Business Administration Office	sba.gov/localresources/district/ok/index.html

Oregon

Oregon State Website	oregon.gov
Information on Starting a Business	oregon.gov/menu_files/business_kut.shtml
Business Structure Filing	filinginoregon.com/business/index.htm
Business Name Registration	filinginoregon.com/business/
Business Tax Registration	oregon.gov/DOR/BUS/index.shtml
City or County Business Licenses	Contact your city or county revenue department
Health Code Requirements and Permits	Contact your city or county health department
Small Business Administration Office	sba.gov/localresources/district/or/index.html

Pennsylvania

Pennsylvania State Website	state.pa.us
Information on Starting a Business	pa.gov/portal/server.pt/community/work/3015
Business Structure Filing	dos.state.pa.us/portal/server.pt/community/corporation_bureau/12457
Business Name Registration	dos.state.pa.us/portal/server.pt/community/corporation_bureau/12457
Business Tax Registration	doreservices.state.pa.us/BusinessTax/PA100/FormatSelection.htm
City or County Business Licenses	Contact your city or county revenue department
Health Code Requirements and Permits	Contact your city or county health department
Small Business Administration Office	sba.gov/localresources/district/pa/

Puerto Rico

Puerto Rico State Website	topuertorico.org/government.shtml
Information on Starting a Business	gobierno.pr/G2B/Inicio/Inicio
Business Structure Filing	pr.gov/Estado/inicio/corporaciones.htm
Business Name Registration	pr.gov/Estado/inicio/marcas.htm
Business Tax Registration	hacienda.gobierno.pr/downloads/pdf/formularios/AS%202914.1.pdf
City or County Business Licenses	Contact your city or county revenue department
Health Code Requirements and Permits	Contact Department of Health for guidelines
Small Business Administration Office	sba.gov/localresources/district/pr/index.html

South Carolina

South Carolina State Website	sc.gov
Information on Starting a Business	sc.gov/business/Pages/default.aspx
Business Structure Filing	scsos.com/Business_Filings/Business_Filings_-_General_Information
Business Name Registration	Not required of domestic businesses
Business Tax Registration	scbos.sc.gov/
City or County Business Licenses	Contact your city or county revenue department
Health Code Requirements and Permits	Contact your city or county health department
Small Business Administration Office	sba.gov/localresources/district/sc/index.html

South Dakota

South Dakota State Website	sd.gov
Information on Starting a Business	sd.gov/servicedirect/
Business Structure Filing	sdsos.gov/busineservices/corporations.shtm
Business Name Registration	sdsos.gov/busineservices/fictitiousbusnames.shtm
Business Tax Registration	apps.sd.gov/applications/rv23cedar/main/main.aspx
City or County Business Licenses	Contact your city or county revenue department
Health Code Requirements and Permits	Contact your city or county health department
Small Business Administration Office	sba.gov/localresources/district/sd/index.html

Tennessee

Tennessee State Website	tennessee.gov
Information on Starting a Business	tennesseeanytime.org/business/index.html
Business Structure Filing	state.tn.us/sos/bus_svc/forms.htm
Business Name Registration	state.tn.us/sos/bus_svc/corporations.htm
Business Tax Registration	tennesseeanytime.org/bizreg/
City or County Business Licenses	Contact your city or county revenue department
Health Code Requirements and Permits	Contact your city or county health department
Small Business Administration Office	sba.gov/localresources/district/tn/index.html

Texas

Texas State Website	texas.gov
Information on Starting a Business	texas.gov/en/discover/Pages/topic.aspx?topicid=%2Fbusiness%2Fstart
Business Structure Filing	Registration depends on business structure
Business Name Registration	Registration depends on business structure
Business Tax Registration	cpa.state.tx.us/taxpermit/
City or County Business Licenses	Contact your city or county revenue department
Health Code Requirements and Permits	Contact your city or county health department
Small Business Administration Office	sba.gov/localresources/district/tx/

US Virgin Islands

US Virgin Islands Website	ltg.gov.vi
Information on Starting a Business	dlca.vi.gov/
Business Structure Filing	ltg.gov.vi/corporations-and-trademarks.html
Business Name Registration	ltg.gov.vi/downloads/forms/TRADENAMECERTIFICATE.pdf
Business Tax Registration	viirb.com/
City or County Business Licenses	Contact your local revenue department
Health Code Requirements and Permits	Contact Department of Health for guidelines

Utah

Utah State Website	utah.gov
Information on Starting a Business	business.utah.gov/
Business Structure Filing	corporations.utah.gov/
Business Name Registration	corporations.utah.gov/
Business Tax Registration	secure.utah.gov/osbr-user/user/welcome.html
City or County Business Licenses	Contact your city or county revenue department
Health Code Requirements and Permits	Contact your city or county health department
Small Business Administration Office	sba.gov/localresources/district/ut/index.html

Vermont

Vermont State Website	vermont.gov
Information on Starting a Business	vermont.gov/portal/business/
Business Structure Filing	sec.state.vt.us/corps/corpindex.htm
Business Name Registration	sec.state.vt.us/corps/forms/tradeapp.htm
Business Tax Registration	vermont.gov/portal/business/index.php?id=91
City or County Business Licenses	Contact your city or county revenue department
Health Code Requirements and Permits	Contact your city or county health department
Small Business Administration Office	sba.gov/localresources/district/vt/index.html

Virginia

Virginia State Website	virginia.gov
Information on Starting a Business	virginia.gov/cmsportal3/business_4096/
Business Structure Filing	scc.virginia.gov/clk/begin.aspx
Business Name Registration	Depends on business structure
Business Tax Registration	tax.virginia.gov/site.cfm?alias=BusinessHome
City or County Business Licenses	Contact your city or county revenue department
Health Code Requirements and Permits	Contact your city or county health department
Small Business Administration Office	sba.gov/localresources/district/va/index.html

Washington

Washington State Website	access.wa.gov
Information on Starting a Business	access.wa.gov/business/start.aspx
Business Structure Filing	sos.wa.gov/corps/Default.aspx
Business Name Registration	dol.wa.gov/business/faqtradename.html
Business Tax Registration	dor.wa.gov/content/doingbusiness/registermybusiness/
City or County Business Licenses	Contact your city or county revenue department
Health Code Requirements and Permits	Contact your city or county health department
Small Business Administration Office	sba.gov/localresources/district/wa/index.html

West Virginia

West Virginia State Website	wv.gov
Information on Starting a Business	wv.gov/business/Pages/StartingaBusiness.aspx
Business Structure Filing	sos.wv.gov/Pages/default.aspx
Business Name Registration	sos.wv.gov/Pages/default.aspx
Business Tax Registration	wva.state.wv.us/wvtax/default.aspx
City or County Business Licenses	Contact your city or county revenue department
Health Code Requirements and Permits	Contact your city or county health department
Small Business Administration Office	sba.gov/localresources/district/wv/index.html

Wisconsin

Wisconsin State Website	wisconsin.gov
Information on Starting a Business	wisconsin.gov/state/core/business.html
Business Structure Filing	wdfi.org/corporations/forms/
Business Name Registration	wisconsin.gov/state/byb/name.html
Business Tax Registration	revenue.wi.gov/faqs/pcs/btr-on.html
City or County Business Licenses	Contact your city or county revenue department
Health Code Requirements and Permits	Contact your city or county health department
Small Business Administration Office	sba.gov/localresources/district/wi/index.html

Wyoming

Wyoming State Website	wyoming.gov
Information on Starting a Business	wyomingbusiness.org/business/txt_starting.htm
Business Structure Filing	soswy.state.wy.us/Forms/FormsFiling.aspx ?startwith=Business
Business Name Registration	soswy.state.wy.us/Forms/FormsFiling.aspx ?startwith=Business
Business Tax Registration	revenue.state.wy.us/PortalVBVS/ DesktopDefault.aspx?tabindex=2&tabid=9
City or County Business Licenses	Contact your city or county revenue department
Health Code Requirements and Permits	Contact your city or county health department
Small Business Administration Office	sba.gov/localresources/district/wy/index.html

ACKNOWLEDGEMENTS

When my first food business book was published in February of 2011, I thought that my writing days were done for a while and it was time to turn my energy back to my much-ignored husband. However, time and time again I was asked by aspiring food truck entrepreneurs about what they needed to know in order to start the food truck of their dreams. Interestingly enough, despite the food truck phenomenon sweeping North America, there are very few comprehensive resources available to anyone who wants to start a food truck, food cart, or food trailer. Motivated as much by their curiosity and energy as by my own, I started researching the ins and outs of mobile food businesses. As such, I must first thank the aspiring mobile food entrepreneurs who contacted me as it was their questions that prompted me to write this second book.

I must also thank Brenda Sciamanna who went above and beyond by spending several hours with me talking through some of the specific issues she faced when starting up her food truck in Lincoln County, PA. She was a pioneer in the food truck business starting back in the early '90s and shared with me some wonderful and very funny stories.

Once again I have to thank my parents who, years ago, were ok with my going from an undergraduate education to culinary school and, later, transitioning to business school. It makes for an eclectic resume but they have supported me throughout and I believe those experiences were all critical in getting me to where I am today.

A huge thank you to my editor Tamara Miller, who took her red pen to this book and read through it to make sure that everything was succinct, spelled correctly and had the appropriate grammar. Who would have guessed that the best way to meet a great editor is on the ski slopes! I very much appreciate all the time and care she took with this book.

There was never any doubt that Michelle Draeger of mdraeger design would design this second book jacket since she so brilliantly captured the feeling I was shooting for with the first book. She has an innate ability to take the picture I have in my head but can't accurately describe and turn it into a show-stopping design.

I continue to be grateful to the professors at the Kellogg School of Management at Northwestern University who took a chance by accepting a pastry chef into their program and were able to turn me into a businesswoman. The wide range of amazing life and work experiences my classmates brought to the classroom also added immeasurably to my education and for that I thank them.

Lastly, I want to thank Bryan, Greta, and Tyr.

I invite you to join me in talking about all the ups, down, concerns, and issues small food businesses face at smallfoodbiz.com.

CPSIA information can be obtained at www.ICGtesting.com
Printed in the USA
LVOW051403030612

284438LV00001B/86/P